Charlemagne

LANCASTER PAMPHLETS

Charlemagne

P. D. King

METHUEN · LONDON

First published in 1986 by
Methuen & Co. Ltd
11 New Fetter Lane
London EC4P 4EE

© *1986 P. D. King*

Typeset in Great Britain by
Scarborough Typesetting Services
and printed by
Richard Clay (The Chaucer Press)
Bungay, Suffolk

British Library Cataloguing in
Publication Data

King, P.D.
Charlemagne. – (Lancaster pamphlets)
1. Charlemagne, Emperor of the West
2. France – Kings and rulers –
Biography
I. Title   II. Series
940.1' 4' 0924   DC73

ISBN 0–416–37350–X

Contents

TO RUSTY

who has a family interest . . .

Foreword

Lancaster Pamphlets offer concise and up-to-date accounts of major historical topics, primarily for the help of students preparing for Advanced Level examinations, though they should also be of value to those pursuing introductory courses in universities and other institutions of higher education. They do not rely on prior textbook knowledge. Without being all-embracing, their aims are to bring some of the central themes or problems confronting students and teachers into sharper focus than the textbook writer can hope to do; to provide the reader with some of the results of recent research which the textbook may not embody; and to stimulate thought about the whole interpretation of the topic under discussion.

At the end of this pamphlet is a list of the recent or fairly recent works that the writer considers most relevant to the subject.

Campaigns and other matters

Saxons and north

808 Danes and Wiltzites attack Abodrites; Franks attack Danes' Slav allies
809 Abodrites attack Wiltzites; Franks move north of Elbe
810 Danes attack Frisia and threaten Saxony; death of Godofrid.

Elsewhere

769 Aquitanian campaign
770 Lombard marriage
773 Lombard campaign
774 Fall of Pavia; C becomes king of Lombards
776 Rodgaud of Fruili's revolt crushed
778 Spanish campaign
781 Tassilo renews oaths; Byzantine marriage alliance
785 Bavarian victory at Bolzano; Gerona accepts Frankish authority
787 Beneventan campaign; Tassilo forced to submit
788 Byzantine marriage alliance collapses; Grimoald made duke of Benevento; Tassilo deposed; Avar attacks on Bavaria and Italy defeated; Byzantines defeated in Calabria
791 Avar campaign
792 Pippin the Hunchback's conspiracy
793 Saracens attack Septimania
795 Avar ring plundered
796 Avar ring replundered
799 Balearics accept Frankish authority .
801 Barcelona captured
805 Bohemian campaign
806 Bohemian campaign; Pamplona accepts Frankish authority; fighting (till 809) with Byzantines

Other matters

768 Accession of C and Carloman; accession of pope Stephen III (d. 772)
771 Death of Carloman
772 Accession of pope Hadrian I (d. 795)
774 First Rome visit; Donation of Charlemagne
775 Death of emperor Constantine V; accession of Leo IV
779 Capitulary of Herstal
780 Death of Leo IV; Irene holds regency for Constantine VI

Simplified genealogical table of
principal personages

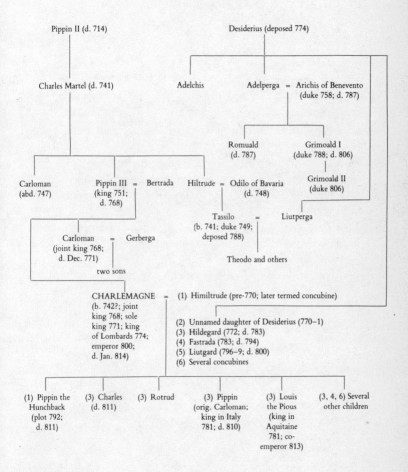

Pippin II (d. 714)

Desiderius (deposed 774)

Charles Martel (d. 741)

Adelchis

Adelperga = Arichis of Benevento
(duke 758; d. 787)

Romuald
(d. 787)

Grimoald I
(duke 788; d. 806)

Grimoald II
(duke 806)

Carloman
(abd. 747)

Pippin III =
(king 751;
d. 768)

Bertrada

Hiltrude = Odilo of Bavaria
(d. 748)

Tassilo =
(b. 741; duke 749;
deposed 788)

Liutperga

Theodo and others

Carloman =
(joint king 768;
d. Dec. 771)

Gerberga

two sons

CHARLEMAGNE =
(b. 742?; joint
king 768; sole
king 771; king
of Lombards 774;
emperor 800;
d. Jan. 814)

(1) Himiltrude (pre-770; later termed concubine)

(2) Unnamed daughter of Desiderius (770–1)
(3) Hildegard (772; d. 783)
(4) Fastrada (783; d. 794)
(5) Liutgard (796–9; d. 800)
(6) Several concubines

(1) Pippin the
Hunchback
(plot 792;
d. 811)

(3) Charles
(d. 811)

(3) Rotrud

(3) Pippin
(orig. Carloman;
king in Italy
781; d. 810)

(3) Louis
the Pious
(king in
Aquitaine
781; co-
emperor 813)

(3, 4, 6) Several
other children

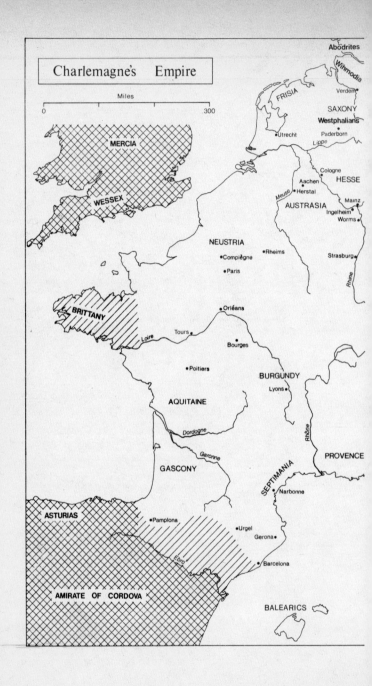

Charlemagne's Empire

Miles
0   300

MERCIA

WESSEX

BRITTANY

NEUSTRIA
• Compiègne   • Rheims
• Paris

Orléans •

Tours •
Loire

Bourges •

• Poitiers

BURGUNDY
Lyons •

AQUITAINE

Dordogne

Garonne

GASCONY

PROVENCE

SEPTIMANIA
• Narbonne

ASTURIAS

• Pamplona

• Urgel
Gerona •

Ebro

• Barcelona

AMIRATE OF CORDOVA

BALEARICS

Abodrites
Wihmodia

FRISIA

SAXONY
Westphalians
• Utrecht   Paderborn
Lippe

Cologne •
Aachen •   HESSE
• Herstal
Meuse   Mainz •
AUSTRASIA   Ingelheim •
              Worms •

Strasburg •

Rhine

Rhône

Charlemagne

Introduction

No figure from the middle ages has impressed himself more powerfully and enduringly upon the consciousness of posterity than Charlemagne. All but a legend in his own lifetime, when already he was 'Charles the Great' – in Latin, 'Carolus Magnus', whence the Old French 'Charlemagne'· – he became one literally within decades of his death. Medieval monarchs looked back to him with reverence: he was the inspiration of Otto III, who opened Charlemagne's tomb to honour him in the year of expected cataclysm, 1000; Frederick Barbarossa had him canonized in 1165; the Capetian kings of France tapped the asset of his blood. Unsurprisingly, he appeared as one of the three Christian representatives among the Nine Worthies of the World. In the sixteenth century Dürer depicted him as the symbol of German imperial majesty; in the seventeenth French admiration expressed itself in his comparison with Louis XIV. Napoleon was hailed as Charlemagne reborn and the German empire proclaimed in 1871 was seen as a successor to the holy Roman empire which he was held to have established (and which Napoleon had ended). In more modern times he has enjoyed a remarkably favourable press among major historians and rarely met with more than shallow disparagement from lesser figures, save in inter-war Germany, where some savaged him as the oppressor of the 'pure' Germanic Saxons and the agent of 'Roman internationalism'. Nowadays, Germans and Frenchmen alike regard him as a father of their countries; at the same time a prize for services to European unity is named after him.

That source-material allowing us to explore the reality of Charlemagne's reign is relatively abundant is itself testimony to his high reputation – as also to one of his achievements, his success in encouraging the use of the written word. Among the sources, two groups require preliminary comment. First, there are annals, year-by-year accounts which furnish the bulk of our narrative material. Basic are the *Annals of the Kingdom of the Franks* (cited as *AKF*), a semi-official record, of composite authorship, compiled during the reign; alongside this stands, for the period to 801, a substantially revised version, often more revealing, produced early in the next reign. In what follows, 'the annalist' designates an author of the first, 'the reviser' the composer of the second.

Second, there are capitularies. It is impossible to define these more exactly than as documents somehow expressive of the governmental will. A capitulary may record a solemn act of state, take the form of a circular directive letter, constitute a memorandum of instruction for those whom Charlemagne dispatched to ensure his will was done, the *missi* (the 'sent ones'), contain additions to a law-code, represent the decisions reached at general assemblies, and so forth. The content may be religious, secular or mixed, of limited or general application.

Among other sources, biographies, in particular the life of Charlemagne by Einhard, a former courtier, that of his son, Louis the Pious, by the anonymous 'Astronomer' and the biographies contained in the *Book of the Popes*, deserve special mention, together with letters, notably those of the scholar Alcuin and of the popes. But much else makes its contribution. There emerges a picture of the reign shadowy in numerous features but clear in its broad outlines and sufficiently extensive to oblige a selective approach in this pamphlet.

The historical background

The religious, social and politico-geographical foundations of the Frankish future were laid in the sixty years following the death in 480 of the last western Roman emperor before Charlemagne himself. The achievements of Clovis (d. 511) were remarkable, and the expansionist impetus he bequeathed was maintained by his immediate successors. After the mid-sixth century, however, Frankish energies turned increasingly to civil war. The beneficiaries were the magnates; and in the seventh-century conflicts it was they who dominated while the kings, Clovis's descendants, became background figures, politically impotent if still politically necessary, such was the respect commanded by their Merovingian blood. At Tertry in 687 the duke of the Austrasians, or east Franks, crushed his opponents in battle and thereafter, until his death in 714, exercised the supreme power in the kingdom. He was of distinguished stock on both sides; but more important to his success will have been his extensive lands, chiefly in the Meuse-Mosel region. This duke was Pippin II (miscalled 'of Herstal'), and he was Charlemagne's great-grandfather.

Pippin's 'reign' is poorly known, but was certainly marked by vigorous military activity, the hallmark of that of the son who eventually succeeded to his power, Charles, later dubbed 'Martel' ('the Hammer'). Campaigning was the more important since it brought wealth, in booty if not in land; and wealth was the material basis of strong lordship. Charles fought external peoples like the Saxons and even expanded into Frisia. But more significantly he reasserted or strengthened central control internally, aided by his success against the Muslims, who had launched themselves at Spain in 711, swiftly destroyed the Christian Visigothic kingdom and soon begun to penetrate north of the Pyrenees. In 732 Charles won a famous victory at Poitiers, which served to cast him in the role of Christian champion.

He was far from this in his distribution of bishoprics and abbacies to his supporters, often laymen, and his massive confiscations of church lands, often bestowed on his vassals – men personally pledged to his service – as grants held conditionally on loyal fulfilment of their obligations, usually military. But he did support missionary activity, led by Willibrord, Boniface and other Anglo-Saxons. Christian duty was not his sole motivation. Christianization within the kingdom promised to engender greater unity and stability, not least because the faith taught (*Romans* 13: 1–2, for example) that God appointed those in authority and required obedience to them. As for outsiders, it was not just that conversion might make them less likely to wage war against coreligionists. Christianity was the Frankish ideology, and we are familiar enough in our own times with the association of ideological imperialism and political control. To Charles, the missionaries were agents of his and Frankish power. But they were agents of another authority also: that of the papacy. Boniface and his fellows worked with papal sanction, looked constantly to Rome and were imbued with the deep devotion to St Peter and his heirs, the popes, characteristic of the Anglo-Saxons, who venerated pope Gregory I (d. 604) as the apostle of England. The Roman influence which they spread became more profound under Pippin III ('the Short') and his brother, who succeeded their father in 741, dividing the kingdom between them just as the sons

3

of Merovingian kings had customarily done, for these were genuinely pious rulers, and in the movement of religious reform which now stirred the kingdom it was again Boniface who was the leading spirit. The increasingly reverential attitude to Rome is exemplified in the clergy's declaration in 747 – the year of Pippin's brother's abdication to become a monk – of their subjection to St Peter and his vicar.

This 'Romanization' was of fundamental importance, indeed a precondition of the papacy's giant step in abandoning the empire which had always been its home and committing itself to the west, an act of incalculable consequence for the future of Europe. The papacy had long been locked in an irreconcilable ideological struggle, usually latent but occasionally exploding into violent life, with the emperors. Papal ideology, developed back in the late fourth and fifth centuries, maintained: first, that Christ, in founding His church, had entrusted its government – the power of 'binding and loosing' in the juridical language of the essential biblical passage, *Matthew* 16: 18–19 – to Peter; second, that He had guaranteed automatic heavenly confirmation of Peter's decisions, third, that the popes, however personally unworthy, were Peter's heirs in office and therefore possessed of identical authority over the church – that is, the community of Christians. Papal history is impossible to comprehend unless the awesome magnitude of these claims is grasped.

But Rome was an imperial city. Notwithstanding popular conviction, the Roman empire did not fall in the fifth century; indeed, in the sixth it re-established its power in the west, where the fifth *had* seen it extinguished. When Tertry was fought the emperor – with his capital at Constantinople and by this stage usually termed Byzantine – still held substantial Italian lands: Sicily and part of the south, the northeastern regions, including Ravenna, where his governor, the exarch, resided, and the duchy of Rome. And the emperors were themselves convinced of their divine appointment and absolute governmental competence. Since nothing was more essential to the empire's welfare than ensuring that God was not angered, it was manifestly their duty to make and enforce the decisions on matters involving the faith. Religion was too important to be left to the clerics. In short, popes asserted supreme authority over the church, which embraced emperors; emperors asserted it over their subjects, who included popes.

By 700 proof of the emperors' determination to make their authority prevail, by force if needs be, and of the hopelessness of anticipating imperial surrender to the papal viewpoint was abundant. Papal bitterness and frustration at the inability to exercise God-given rights was acute. But there was nothing to do, nowhere to turn. The papacy could not go it alone, not least for fear of the Lombards, who occupied much of Italy and had greedy eyes (the popes thought) on Rome. The vital importance of the Frankish developments was that they opened up the possibility of an escape route from what has been called the papacy's 'Byzantine captivity'. The complex combination of circumstances which moved the popes along this path, not without many hesitations, cannot be examined here. Essential, however, was the espousal of iconoclasm, a movement attacking the veneration of religious images, by the emperor Leo III (717–41). Pope Gregory II (715–31) opposed him, denouncing iconoclasm as heretical, rejecting his right to pronounce on the matter and warning of western readiness to fight in defence of St Peter and images. As the dispute progressed Leo stripped the papacy of certain jurisdictional rights and – a devastating blow – confiscated its vast southern Italian and Sicilian estates. To economic pressure was added military, for the Lombards appeared more menacing by the minute. And it was for aid against them that in 739 Pope Gregory III (731–41) appealed to Charles Martel, to whom he also declared his willingness to secede from the empire.

Charles did not respond, but the episode is a signpost to the 750s, a revolutionary decade. Three matters demand attention. The first is the deposition of the Merovingian Childeric III and the elevation of Pippin III, Charlemagne's father, to kingship in 751. Important enough in itself, this step had been preceded by a mission to gain papal sanction – telling testimony to Frankish respect – and Zachary (741–52) had 'commanded by virtue of apostolic authority that Pippin should be made king' (*AKF*). Papal involvement in kingmaking was unprecedented. So, among the Franks, was the anointing associated with the elevation; its purpose will have been to furnish Pippin, who lacked the charisma of Merovingian blood, with his own, greater, charisma, that of God's grace. The second is the conclusion of a papal-Frankish 'alliance' following the first-ever papal crossing of the Alps in 753, just forty-three years after the last-ever papal journey to Constantinople. The trip, by Stephen II (752–7), was occasioned by the increased threat to Rome after the Lombards' recent capture of Ravenna and most of the Byzantine north-east. In Francia in 754 Pippin promised to recover these lands from the Lombards and to hand them over to the papacy. Almost certainly he was persuaded to this undertaking by a celebrated forgery, exposed only centuries later, the Donation of Constantine, which asserted *inter alia* that Constantine (d. 337) – the first Christian emperor – had given Italy and the west to pope Silvester (d. 335). In return Stephen forbade the choice of a king from any other family, re-anointed Pippin, anointed his two sons to kingship and bestowed the title of 'patrician of the Romans' on all three to indicate their role as the papacy's military protectors. The third is the consequence of campaigns of 755 and 756 which brought the Lombard king to heel. 'Pippin conquered Ravenna with Pentapolis and the whole exarchate and handed it over to St Peter' (*AKF*). The papal state, economically vital, had been created – by a Frank who owed his kingship to one pope, campaigned at the behest of another and exercised his largesse at the ultimate expense of the empire, of whose rulers the popes had always been subjects.

Whether Charles was born in 742, the conventional date, assumed correct here, or in 747, as some hold, his boyhood years were, then, scarcely uneventful. And there still lay ahead the great enterprise of the 760s, the subjection of long-autonomous Aquitaine by ruthless and almost annual campaigning. The expedition of 768 saw the death of Waifar, the enemy leader, and resistance all but crushed. But on his return the triumphant Pippin was struck down by illness. Reaching St-Denis, he was able to make provision for the customary division before death claimed him. Like many another able father he has languished somewhat in the shadow of his exceptional son. On 9 October 768, the same day that saw the elevation of his younger brother Carloman at Soissons, Charles was raised to the kingship at Noyon. One of the most celebrated reigns of history had begun.

The early years, 768–81

CHARLES AND CARLOMAN, 768–71

The years of shared rule are a dark period. Nevertheless, it is clear that relations between Charles and his brother were normally hostile. For what it is worth, they both sent clerics, at papal request, to participate in a Roman council, held in April 769. But a breach is already apparent from events that year in Aquitaine, where Charles directed the first of his numerous campaigns as king against a rebellion led by Hunald, perhaps Waifar's son. His force was small but sufficed to snuff out the rising in the spring, and although Hunald escaped into Gascony, the threat of invasion by a larger force which Charles marched down to the

Dordogne, coupled with the construction of a fortress there and a demonstration across the Garonne, persuaded the Gascon leader to surrender the refugee and himself acknowledge Charles's overlordship. Already in this episode we perceive some of the qualities which made Charles such an outstandingly successful warleader: swiftness and daring of initial response; determination to press matters to an advantageous conclusion; care to assemble substantial forces to achieve this objective; forcefulness of threat and demand; appreciation of the importance of strongholds.

Now, although a reliable contemporary source reports that the division gave part of Aquitaine to Carloman, he did not campaign. The brothers met in Aquitaine after Charles's first expedition, but Carloman returned abruptly home. The reviser and Einhard together give us to understand that he had promised assistance but been prevented from rendering it by 'evil counsel'. Sparing the ruler by blaming the adviser is a familiar device, but this is perhaps the truth; his Aquitanian territories may have remained quiet and his magnates declined to provoke trouble and risk all on another's behalf. The German scholar Martin Lintzel, however, hypothesized that Carloman did not campaign because 769 saw Charles's seizure of his portion of Aquitaine. Though unprovable, his thesis has the merit of explaining the reviser's concern to assert twice in six lines that Aquitaine had fallen to Charles in the original division; there were skeletons in the family cupboard, and his was an attempt to doublelock the door.

The reconciliation which followed was shortlived, and everything suggests that Pippin's widow, Bertrada, who seems to have arranged it, was not the evenhanded motherly mediator of the conventional view. It was certainly as a partisan of her elder son that she travelled to Bavaria and Italy in 770. The outcome was the formation of a sort of triple *entente* between Charles, Desiderius, the Lombard king, and Tassilo of Bavaria; the last was already a son-in-law of Desiderius and now Charles became another. In view of the breach between Pippin III and Tassilo (p. 18), Pippin's Lombard campaigns and Charles's own later dealings with both his partners, this *entente* has appeared to some to reflect his uncertainty of political touch. Rather, it demonstrates its sureness. The target was patently Carloman, who now had potential enemies on three sides. Pope Stephen III (768–72), initially aghast at a Frankish marriage with the 'most foully stinking' Lombards and threatening excommunication, was placated by territorial and other concessions; and the isolated Carloman could find support only in Desiderius's enemies within Rome. What is often called a pro-Frankish rising there in Lent 771 was actually the work of these men, aided by a group of Carloman's Franks; its collapse before Desiderius's armed force brought papal praise for the king of the papacy's traditional foes.

Charles's ultimate intentions towards his brother can only be guessed at. As it was, Carloman died in December 771 and his kingdom passed peacefully to Charles. Carloman's widow fled with her infant sons and a few magnates to Italy, whither Charles's Lombard wife, outliving her usefulness, had probably been sent packing on first news of the death. One feels that she made the right decision. Charles was never wilfully cruel and was a devoted family man. But he was a politician of his age, aware of the need for constant vigilance and ruthlessness in the suppression of threats. When a bastard conspired against him in 792 he showed fatherly indulgence only to the extent of sentencing him to monastic incarceration while executing his principal supporters. The fate of Carloman's children when they did later fall into their uncle's hands is in fact unknown.

In essaying a periodization of Charlemagne's reign Ganshof drew the first dividing-line at 771 – unquestionably correctly. The demise of Carloman allowed Charles to extend his vision to more distant horizons; the enlargement of power which came with rule of the whole Frankish kingdom gave him the means of advancing towards these, sword in one hand, cross in the other. His energy and decisiveness did the rest. Within eight months of Carloman's death the first of the expansionist enterprises which mark the reign was under way.

SAXONY AND ITALY, 772–7

The first was also the greatest: the conquest of Saxony. The Saxons were an old problem, the revival of which in the eighth century, after generations of relative quiet, is connected with the occupation in *c.* 700 of lands between the Lippe and the Rhine by Westphalians, who thus became immediate neighbours of the Franks. Westphalians were one of the four groups into which the Saxons were divided, the others being Angrarians, Eastphalians and, on both sides of the lower Elbe, Nordliudi, 'north people'. It was with the first three groups, the South Saxons, that Charles was mostly involved. Fiercely independent, the Saxons lacked any permanent central authorities, a feature which will have made dealings with them impossibly difficult and helps to explain why agreements so often failed to stick. The largely open border-terrain gave them every opportunity for raiding, which was endemic. Charles's fore-bears had frequently campaigned against them to punish and plunder, and in 758 Pippin had imposed tribute: 500 oxen in the sixth century, this was now set at 300 horses, reflecting the increased importance of cavalry. Charles's principal reasons in deciding upon conquest will have been to eliminate a long-standing danger, to win renown, to gain treasure and lands with which to reward his followers as a good lord should, and both to please God and to save souls by bringing the Saxons, obdurate pagans, to the faith. The attribution to him of some ideal of unifying the Germanic peoples is fancifully anachronistic.

Despite the reviser's entry for 775, which provides the grounds for the frequent assertion that conquest began only then, it was undoubtedly the aim from the outset. Einhard is specific that the Franks began the war because resolved to have done with mere retaliation, and evidence that the king led a mighty army in 772 and was intent on conversion, to accomplish which he took many clerics with him, is telling. So is the character of the campaign, for Charles struck first at Eresburg, the stronghold guarding southerly access to what German scholars have dubbed *die Weserfestung*, 'fortress Weser', a region of key strategic importance. This was not the soft target of a raider; indeed, it looks as if Charles left a garrison there. From Eresburg the king advanced to the site of the Saxons' great idol, the Irminsul, destroyed this and plundered the shrine of its gold and silver. Such desecration was bound to provoke retaliation if opportunity offered, and could have commended itself only if thoroughgoing conquest and Christianization were in mind. Before withdrawing the king had penetrated to the Weser, where he received hostages.

Undoubtedly Charles intended to press ahead with his Saxon designs in 773. Circumstances dictated otherwise. Early in the year an envoy from pope Hadrian I (772–95) arrived to request aid against Desiderius, who had not only failed to fulfil territorial undertakings but had actually seized papal lands and also demanded that Hadrian anoint Carloman's sons as kings. Papal function would have lent the highest authority to their hereditary claims and made them valuable weapons (Desiderius will have believed) against Charles. Pique at his daughter's repudiation was probably a less important motive than concern to strengthen his position at an opportune moment. Hadrian's biographer declares that Desiderius was bent on the subjection of all Italy. But he was not the stuff of which conquerors are made; threat of excommuni-cation was enough to turn him back when he marched on Rome in 773.

Charles, with Saxon fish to fry, was loth to intervene; moreover, he was uncertain whether to believe Hadrian or Desiderius, whose envoys declared that he had satisfied all the papal claims. Even when Frankish legates, sent to investigate, reported back that Desiderius did hold the disputed territories and had refused to give them up, Charles sought to avoid conflict, offering the Lombard king a large sum to surrender them. Desiderius rejected the proposal: no doubt he took it, rightly, to show Charles's reluctance to fight and calculated, this time wrongly, that the king would not dare, come the crunch, to leave the Saxons a free hand by committing his forces to the south.

Charles followed a favourite strategy of his in dividing his forces for the campaign. But both armies found their passage blocked at the southern defiles of the Alpine passes. Twice Charles proposed peaceful settlement but was refused. Finally a force negotiated the mountains to get behind Desiderius, who promptly retreated to his capital. The Lombards had shut themselves up in their cities and waited for enemies to go home at the end of the campaigning season before; and it was already September. But Charles, whose perseverance was one of his most impressive qualities, declined to play the game and settled down to a winter siege. We know almost nothing of military activity in the following months save that Charles took troops to Verona, where Carloman's widow yielded herself and her sons. Eventually, in June 774, Pavia capitulated. 'And all the Lombards from all the cities of Italy came there and subjected themselves to the dominion of the glorious lord king Charles and the Franks' (*AKF*).

Despite appearances, this does not mean that the Lombards became a subject people of the Franks. The Lombard kingdom retained its identity, Charles simply stepping into Desiderius's shoes. Henceforth his title read: 'Charles, by the grace of God king of the Franks and the Lombards and patrician of the Romans.' In 781 Lombard self-esteem was further gratified when Charles's son, Pippin, was anointed and crowned as king in Italy by Hadrian. (This is the first known coronation among the Franks.) Though there was a gradual Frankish influx, the institutional and social structure was preserved virtually intact. In short, the kingdom went on largely as before; only the king had changed. The northern Lombards accepted the situation passively enough; only one revolt (p. 28) is known. Nor did the problems which threatened from the powerful duchy of Spoleto, in central Italy, materialize. Benevento, to the south, was a different matter (see pp. 28–31).

For Charles, the takeover of the Lombard kingdom was of the very highest moment. Perforce he became sucked into the complex, shifting world of Italian politics, where pope, emperor and local potentates jostled for position and advantage. Without the closer contact with Rome which ensued, the coronation of 800 would be inconceivable, while his new status made him in Byzantine eyes a figure of major importance, to be wooed or opposed as appropriate but always to be reckoned with. Nor should we overlook the broader significance of the conquest. The year 774 marks the pregnant historical moment when begins that persistent, fateful involvement of northern powers in Italy which has dominated and determined so much of its history over the centuries and in no small measure shaped the country of today.

The price of conquest in the south was paid by the north. In 774 the Saxons ravaged deep into Hesse; it took a miracle, men believed, to prevent their burning Boniface's church at Fritzlar, a fitting target of retaliation for the destruction of the Irminsul. Charles arrived back too late to do more than send raiding columns into Saxony but in 775 led a massive host across the Rhine. The campaign was a triumph: the Franks stormed the westerly fortress of Syburg, reoccupied and refortified Eresburg, won a pitched battle on the Weser and forced the submission of Eastphalians, Angrarians and Westphalians in turn. But the king was obliged to go south again early in 776 (p. 28) and when he returned it was to hear that the Saxons were again in arms: Eresburg had been abandoned and the garrison at Syburg attacked. Saxon military capability was not negligible: they had siege-machinery at both fortresses.

The swiftness of Charles's appearance with another huge army stunned the Saxons, who flocked in their thousands to the source of the Lippe, Lippspringe, to submit and promise to become Christians. It would not be surprising if this had been the site of the Irminsul and was deliberately chosen to emphasize the superiority of the Frankish God. It was on the Lippe, too, that he constructed a new fortress named after himself, Karlsburg, where further submissions and baptisms took place. And it was near there, at Paderborn, that he resolved to hold the annual general assembly of his people in 777. His decision reveals that his grip on western Saxony was already firm; the route to Paderborn was evidently secure. It seems certain that this was the ancient way leading from the Rhine by way of Dortmund and probable that it was already protected by a swathe of contiguous estates held by the king's *fideles*, his 'faithful ones'. The purpose in choosing Paderborn is patent: the Saxons were to be shown that his was now the power in the land and to be awed by an imposing demonstration of his might, emphasized by the presence of exotic potentates from Muslim Spain. The outcome was gratifying. Nearly all the Saxons summoned attended and they hastened to take new and more rigorous oaths of allegiance, while there were further baptisms.

The events of 776–7 were seen as epoch-making. One annalist was moved to recall that it was 172 years since the death of Gregory I; evidently he saw the king as completing that pope's work of Saxon conversion. Another made comparison with John the Baptist; a poet drew a parallel with Christ's coming to save the world. The triumph will have had its impact upon Charles too. Hard-headed soldier-statesman though he was, he was also deeply pious, convinced of his duty to do battle as his Lord's *fidelis*, convinced too that it was heavenly decisions which ultimately determined earthly fortunes. What conclusion could be drawn from his extraordinary successes thus far but that God smiled upon the efforts of His loyal warrior? What more comforting than the assurance of divine support! The rudest of shocks lay ahead.

SPAIN AND THE AFTERMATH, 778–81

Charles's Spanish expedition of 778 is customarily seen as the fruit of an understanding between the king and the Muslims attending Paderborn. Two of these men had family reasons for hostility to the ruler of Muslim Spain, the amir of Cordova, and the disaffection of the third, Ibn al-Arabi, governor of Barcelona and probably Gerona, is clear from his surrender of himself and his cities to Charles. But far from contemplating a campaign across the Pyrenees, Charles planned to go to Rome for Easter 778 for papal baptism of his newborn son Carloman (renamed Pippin when Hadrian did baptize him in 781). Only in May did the pope, disappointed at his non-appearance, receive a report from Charles that the Muslims were bent on invasion and that he would be campaigning. The expedition, in other words, was pre-emptive, though that by no means precludes further motives, such as territorial gain and the aiding of Spanish Christians. Whereas Charles is conventionally believed to have invaded in expectation of Ibn al-Arabi's support, the evidence points rather to the latter's having abandoned his allegiance (as a later governor of Barcelona was to do within two years of giving it in 797) and become hostile.

Immense forces took part in the campaign, which saw Charles enter Spain by a western route, attack Pamplona, which surrendered, and receive hostages from Abu Taher, governor of Huesca and perhaps Pamplona itself. A second army marched via Barcelona. Developments at Saragossa, where the two forces united, are unknown, though the city almost certainly did not fall. In late July Charles turned for home, taking Ibn al-Arabi (in fact rescued *en route* by his sons) with him in chains. At Pamplona he destroyed the walls so that it might not rebel. There is no indication of a forced or early withdrawal; nor, given a pre-emptive objective, may one deem the expedition a failure. But it was not yet over. While the king reached Gascony safely, his rearguard, protecting the baggage-train, were less fortunate. On 15 August, somewhere in the western Pyrenees – almost certainly at Roncesvalles – they suffered ambush and destruction by Basques. Everything, including the annalist's total silence, indicates a disaster of the first magnitude. The reviser reports that numerous high-ranking figures were killed, and Einhard names three, including the eponymous hero of the famous *Song of Roland*; the Astronomer, exasperatingly, omits to give names 'since these are widely known'. Christian refugees were soon leaving Spain, but Charles never set foot there again.

The tragedy in the Pyrenees was not all the king had to contend with. On reaching Auxerre he learned that the Saxons were again in revolt: Karlsburg had been destroyed and they were ravaging the Rhineland, committing many atrocities. After the euphoria of 777 this must have come as a terrible shock. How could it be understood except as confirmation of what the Spanish disaster will already have suggested, that God was displeased? Were his achievements in Aquitaine and Italy also perhaps insecure? Ganshof described 778–9 as years of crisis; and whether or not the situation was truly critical, there is good reason to believe that Charles so perceived it.

Necessarily, his response was in important measure military and political. A column dispatched against the Saxon raiders caught and defeated them as they withdrew; and in 779 Charles himself campaigned in Saxony, forcing a general submission. When he went north again, in 780, he encountered no recorded resistance and advanced eastwards, to reach the Elbe for the first time. Both Slavs from across the river and Nordliudi now submitted and were baptized; and Charles established a missionary organization. In Aquitaine, perhaps still in 778, he took the precaution of installing Frankish counts, abbots and vassals, while in 781 he acted to satisfy pride and particularist sentiment by giving the Aquitanians, as he also gave the Lombards (p. 10), their own king. (The Astronomer has a pleasing account of how the three-year-old Louis, born in Aquitaine and, like Pippin, anointed and crowned by Hadrian, was taken down to the Loire in his wooden carrycot and then fitted out with mini-weapons and sat on a horse to take ceremonial possession of his kingdom.) Moreover, Charles's 781 Italian expedition also saw the archbishop of Milan baptize a daughter and stand as her godfather; this not only bound one of the most important clerics in northern Italy to him in spiritual kinship but was calculated to gratify Lombard opinion. Earlier, in 779, the duke of Spoleto had made the long journey to Francia and returned laden with gifts; Charles was perhaps anxious about his fidelity.

Military and political action would be unavailing, however, were God not placated. Between September 778 and May 779 Charles appears hardly to have budged from Herstal, on the Meuse, his favourite early residence, and everything suggests that he spent this period pondering and discussing how he had failed his Lord, how he could regain His support. The duties inherent in true Christian kingship had been much considered and expounded over the centuries, and the views current in Charles's day were long-established and undisputed. He will have been exposed to their influence from childhood. But it was probably only now that they ceased to be commonplaces and took a genuine grip on his mind, with the most profound consequences for the future. Before 778 Charles was the Christian warrior-king; after it, though remaining that, he was also, and increasingly, the Christian reformer and educator, striving for the creation of a just, orderly and harmonious society in which men would live in obedience to God's, and God's appointed officers', commands. His ultimate objective was nothing less than the transformation of society in accordance with Christian teachings – in other words, an ideological 'renewal' or 'rebirth' (to use the language of the day) precisely comparable with that which a number of twentieth-century societies have been meant to undergo (see also p. 33).

The first manifestation of the new spirit was a series of measures agreed in council in March 779 and recorded in what is only the second extant capitulary of the reign. The emphasis here lies on order, system, authority, though justice and morality are concerns also. The ecclesiastical articles opening the capitulary demonstrate the themes: clerics must be subject to episcopal authority, bishops to metropolitan; bishops must be ordained for vacant sees; a cleric from one diocese must not be accepted by the bishop of another; bishops are entitled to dispose of the

14

tithes, which all must pay, and to act against certain sexual offenders; monasteries must live according to their governing rules and abbesses remain resident. Other provisions show a determination to have major criminals brought to book and punished severely, to ensure justice in the courts, to eradicate private armies and blood-vengeance, irreconcilable with the ordered society of Charles's vision. There is a moral dimension to rulings forbidding the sale of slaves beyond the frontiers and group-oaths. The capitulary of Herstal was understandably regarded as a document of fundamental importance, for later capitularies often refer to it; evidently an archive copy was kept. And for us, too, it is of capital value, not just for the light it sheds on contemporary institutions and so forth but also for its revelation of Charles's aims and preoccupations on the morrow of the crisis of 778.

Expansion continued, 782–804

SAXONY, 782–5

As we saw, Saxony was apparently quiet in 780, and it remained so in 781. The time must have seemed ripe for consolidation, and at the general assembly of 782, at Lippspringe, Charles divided the land into counties, the territorial units of local government normal elsewhere, and appointed Saxon counts. Shortly afterwards, back in Francia, he ordered Saxon participation in a campaign against Slav raiders in Frankish Thuringia and Saxony itself. Already at this moment, however, the Saxons were again in revolt, 'at the instigation of Widukind' (*AKF*).

So much has been written with such reverent enthusiasm about Widukind, particularly by German historians in the 1930s, when some evidently saw him as a sort of pre-incarnation of the *Führer*, that it is salutary to remember Lintzel's dampening observation that all the reports concerning him would fill no more than a quarter of a quarto page. We know that Widukind was a pagan and a Westphalian leader; that he was twice, in 777 and 782, absent from general assemblies in Saxony and twice, in 778 and 782, incited the Saxons to rebellion; that after each of these episodes, and in 777, he found refuge among the Danes; and that in 785 he submitted and was baptized (after which he vanishes from sight). He was undoubtedly the leader of Saxon resistance between 778 and 785 and prominent earlier. Virtually nothing else can be said; we cannot even assert that he led the Saxons in battle. The Saxon campaigns have occasioned other theses of rare imaginativeness, one may add; some historians have even felt able to expunge the blood-bath of Verden (see p. 17). One persistent interpretation has it that the Saxon response to Charles was class-based, the nobles cleaving to him out of self-interest, the rest (with whom Widukind, breaking class ranks, threw in his lot) bravely fighting for land and liberty. The appeal of this view, comfortingly tidy, comfortingly supportive of widely held prejudices, is understandable. But the thesis is highly improbable, not least because the nobles' power was such that resistance could scarcely have lasted so long without their participation, let alone against their opposition. That a goodly number of important Saxons did back Charles is certain, however.

Incitement by Widukind cannot stand as a self-sufficient reason for the 782 rising. Perhaps the introduction of the county system, with its prospect of firmer government, caused alarm. But the principal provo-cation was probably the contents of a notorious thirty-four-clause capitulary concerning Saxony. Its date is uncertain, many historians inclining to 777 or 785. But its rulings presuppose a county framework, and the seemingly settled circumstances encouraging Charles to estab-lish the counties in 782 would also explain its issue. It has generated much heat under historical collars, Halphen, for example, writing of its 'unequalled harshness' and 'regime of terror'. It is difficult to see why. The capitulary *was* harsh; but so was Saxon 'national' law, retained in force, which recognized an unusually large number of capital offences. Moreover, its harshness was directed not at Saxons as Saxons but at Saxons as pagans. Only three of the eleven clauses specifying capital crimes deal with secular, public order, offences; the concern of the others is the defence of the Christian cause or the eradication of paganism. Thus, death threatens the man who burns or robs a church, kills a cleric, eats meat in Lent (save of necessity; a priest must investigate), consumes human flesh, cremates a corpse, refuses baptism, performs human sacri-fice or supports pagan hostility to Christians, actively or passively. But death will be avoided, declares another, shrewdly calculated, clause, should an undetected offender make confession to a priest and do penance. Other measures, requiring the Saxons to provide land and slaves for the churches, to pay property and labour tithes, to attend church regularly and so forth, reveal no less clearly Charles's determi-nation to build Saxony into an exclusively Christian land.

Refusal to countenance diversity of belief and associated practice offends modern western susceptibilities, but the historian will not go far without encountering it or get far without eschewing outrage and seeking understanding, for it has been the norm throughout most of European history and is scarcely banished from today's world; there is the closest parallel, indeed, between the attitude to the unbeliever in earlier societies convinced of their possession of Christian truth and that to the dissident in ideologically totalitarian modern societies. Charles would have considered himself failing in his duty both to God and to his Saxon and other subjects, whose welfare depended upon God's benevolence, had he not endeavoured to crush paganism, an affront to the divine majesty, and to advance Christianity. Saxons who accepted the faith and its demands had nothing to fear from the capitulary, which from Charles's standpoint was positively beneficial in that it offered order, civilization and the priceless prospect of salvation. Not surprisingly, many Saxons saw things differently.

The annalist tells how the rebels of 782 were met in the Süntel mountains by the Austrasians marching against the Slavs and worsted, though two important Franks were killed. Heaven knows how scholars would have judged Charles had there been nothing more to go on. The reality, revealed by the reviser, is that the Franks, thanks to glory-seeking commanders and an undisciplined cavalry charge, were slaughtered almost to a man. Among the dead were the king's chamberlain, his constable, four other counts and twenty other nobles. Charles's response was swift and terrible. Advancing into Saxony with a hurriedly gathered army, he received from the Saxon leaders – the counts are doubtless meant – the persons of 4500 rebels and at Verden, in a single day, had every last one put to death. Emotion and calculation probably combined to prompt such extreme action; if the massacre gave vent to rage at the incorrigible perfidy of the Saxons, grief at the loss of old comrades, lust for revenge, it also offered the benefit of removing much of the opposition and, he perhaps thought, of cowing what remained into lasting submission.

If he did think thus, he was badly mistaken. Probably the massacre inflamed the Saxons to fiercer resistance. At any rate, 783 saw the rebels numerous enough to offer Charles pitched battle twice, and although they lost heavily on both occasions, allowing him to ravage to the Elbe, rebellion still gripped Saxony the following year. Again Charles devastated far and wide, again the Franks won in the field. But resistance persisted, and the unprecedented decision was taken to winter in Saxony. From Eresburg the king and his generals led out strike-forces to harry and plunder, capture the strongholds, seize command of the roads; and these tactics succeeded. By summer 785 the land was pacified.

The capitulation of Widukind sealed the triumph; Charles himself stood godfather at his baptism, at Attigny, in Francia, late in 785. The king's work in bringing (or returning) the Saxons to the faith made a deep impression; as in 777, one writer recalled Gregory I, while pope Hadrian decreed three days of litanies throughout the entire Christian world.

The satisfaction one can sense behind the annalist's laconic 'And then all Saxony was subjugated' was justified. It was; and it remained so for seven years, a period which saw Charles engaged in a new theatre of operations – the south-east – against, first, Tassilo, and, second, the Avars.

TASSILO

Tassilo, born in 741, stemmed from the hereditary ducal family of Bavaria, a region much larger than its recent namesake, since including modern Austria to east of Salzburg. But it was by the decision of Pippin III, his uncle, who had managed to reassert a degree of central authority over the duchy, formally part of the kingdom but in past practice often autonomous, that he was installed as duke in 749. In 757, on coming of age, Tassilo attended the Compiègne assembly and there commended himself in vassalage, swearing numerous oaths of lifelong fidelity to Pippin and his sons on the relics of Denis, Martin and other Frankish saints. Pippin should perhaps have included the odd Bavarian saint, however; in 763 Tassilo abandoned him on campaign and abjured his obedience as a vassal. The king's long struggle with Waifar, with whom Tassilo perhaps allied, prevented counteraction, but the duke was probably lucky in the timing of Pippin's death. Bavaria's omission from the 768 division indicates its effective independence.

It is often assumed that Charles was looking to settle his father's account by overthrowing Tassilo from the outset, but that other commitments and the duke's strength obliged a long wait. What scant information there is rather suggests his contentment with their relationship (whatever its terms may have been) for a decade and more after 768. These years yield no evidence of opposition. The contacts in 770 were mentioned above (p. 7); it was about then, too, that abbot Sturm, as Charles's envoy to Tassilo, 'established friendship between them for many years', in his biographer's words. It is perhaps unlikely that Hadrian would have baptized Tassilo's son, Theodo, in 772 had he known Charles would be upset. Bavarians participated in the one

18

campaign, the Spanish, where we know the composition of Charles's forces. That important figures in Bavaria looked primarily to the king need not imply their or his hostility to the duke; in the sub-kingdoms Charles had his men, his sons theirs. Again, nothing argues that Tassilo's vigorous religious policy, marked by monastic foundations, support for missionary work and conciliar activity, or his victory over the Carantanian Slavs in 772 and the prestige he gained thereby worried or offended Charles.

In 781, however, king and pope sent a joint embassy to impress upon Tassilo that he must observe his oaths; and the duke appeared at Worms, renewed his oaths and gave hostages as surety for future obedience. It is a Bavarian source which reports Tassilo's sour response to an earlier refusal by Charles to allow all the members of a large ducal embassy passage to Rome and adds that Charles feared the duke's aim was to surpass his might, that Tassilo was indeed colluding with Saxons, Slavs and Avars, the king's enemies, and that war was prevented only by papal mediation, bringing the Worms meeting and 'eternal peace'. Tassilo seems to have been the one looking for trouble. On the other hand, Charles may well have shown a new insistence on Tassilo's observance of his oaths because of his pious stocktaking in 778–9 (p. 14).

However that may be, the events of 781 certainly provide no grounds for believing Charles bent on Tassilo's destruction; indeed, it was probably now that territories detached from Bavaria many decades before were restored. Equally, the duke's disgruntlement at being recalled to strict obedience is a likelier cause of the hostility which evidently followed than aggressive intent by Charles. As regards events, we hear only of fighting in the Tyrol, initiated by Charles's commander in Italy in the belief that Tassilo was conspiring with Widukind and culminating in a Bavarian victory at Bolzano in 785. When Tassilo's envoys, in Rome in 787, requested papal mediation between king and duke, Charles assured Hadrian that he had long sought peace and proposed immediate settlement. Hadrian's fierce reaction to the envoys' refusal, on the grounds that they dare not commit Tassilo, argues that Charles was making no new demands; the pope imposed excommunication on the duke and his supporters should he break his past promises, charged him to obedience to Charles in all things and warned that the blame would be his should bloodshed occur. Tassilo promised accordingly; but he did not attend the 787 Worms assembly, and when Charles instructed him to fulfil what the pope and righteousness alike required and appear before him he spurned the command.

The king now resorted to a massive show of force. Advancing with one army to near Augsburg, he ordered another to Pföring, on the Danube, and a third to Bolzano. According to the annalist, the Bavarians recognized that right was on Charles's side. At all events, Tassilo capitulated without a fight and came to the king. The most striking feature of what followed is that he did not suffer deposition; he handed over the duchy but then received it back again. The surrender was evidently required as a public demonstration that he was duke by royal commission, not by inherent right. Tassilo also gave himself in vassalage to the king, acknowledged his sins and misdeeds, renewed his oaths yet again and delivered hostages, including Theodo. Given all this, and what lay ahead, the hypothesis that Charles refrained from deposition because he felt insufficiently strong looks positively perverse. Not Tassilo's overthrow but his loyalty was what the king sought.

He did not obtain it and in 788 Tassilo, attending the Ingelheim assembly, found himself on trial for his life, accused of breach of fidelity. Specific charges included conspiring with the Avars, seeking the lives of royal vassals, encouraging perjury towards the king and himself committing it. He was found guilty on all counts and those present – Franks, Bavarians, Lombards, Saxons and others – 'remembering his earlier evil deeds and how he had deserted the lord king Pippin on campaign' (*AKF*), unanimously declared that he should die. It was probably now that Tassilo confessed, in a bid for clemency. This he received: mercy was a prime virtue of the Christian king; besides, he was Charles's kinsman. Dispatched to a monastery, the former duke was to be trotted out in 794 before the synodists at Frankfurt (p. 36) to beg pardon for his past sins and to renounce all his family's Bavarian rights and properties. It was a humiliating end for a proud dynasty. The charges against Tassilo have sometimes been deemed trumped-up. But that is a judgement unsupported by evidence, highly implausible in view of Charles's moderation in 787 and directly contradicted by the report in the *AKF* that Tassilo was the instigator of the attacks launched against Italy and Bavaria in 788 by the Avars.

THE AVARS, 788–97

The Avars, an Asiatic people, had settled in Pannonia (broadly, western Hungary and eastern Austria) in *c.* 570 and had their heyday in the following decades when they and their numerous Slav subjects spread an unprecedented devastation and terror throughout the Balkans. (A Slav speciality was anal impaling.) But a failed onslaught on Constantinople in 626 had led to the disintegration of their empire and thereafter they had kept themselves much to themselves. Tassilo seems to have been on generally friendly terms with his eastern neighbours and concluded an alliance with them at the time of the Tyrol conflict. There is probably more to their attacks in 788 than meets the eye. Relations between Charles and Constantinople collapsed in 787–8, and imperial troops launched a major assault in southern Italy late in 788 (p. 31). There is every possibility that Tassilo, the Avars and the Byzantines were acting in concert; indeed, the *AKF* as good as say as much. They also hold Tassilo's Lombard wife, Liutperga, a villainess in the piece. This makes sense: she had every reason to hate Charles, who had repudiated her sister and deposed her father (pp. 8, 10); another sister, Adelperga, widow of the duke of Benevento, urged imperial intervention; her brother, Adelchis, was a key figure in the Byzantine plans; Lombard–Avar friendship was traditional.

The Avars were defeated, however, and when they returned in greater force again lost the day. Charles went to Regensburg in late 788 to arrange border defence against them and perhaps at this time appointed Gerold, brother of his former wife, Hildegard (d. 783), as governor of Bavaria. But he appears to have envisaged neither an offensive against the Avars nor pressing danger from them, for in 789 he was on campaign east of the Elbe, forcing the (temporary) submission of the Wiltzite Slavs, whose long-standing hostility to the Franks and their allies, like the Slavic Abodrites, had prompted his attack. In 790, unusually, he did not campaign at all. But trouble with the Avars was already brewing, the issue being the location of the borders. Negotiations failed to achieve a settlement and, though no source states it explicitly, the Avars almost certainly proceeded, still in 790, to assert their standpoint by force. At any rate, Charles sent the largest part of his army to Bavaria against them in 790, and in 791, when he took the offensive, the purpose was to revenge 'immense and intolerable evil . . . perpetrated against the holy church and the Christian people' (*AKF*).

The Christian ambience of this war was indeed very marked. It has to be seen against the background of the recent crises facing Charles – the Bavarian–Avar–Beneventan–imperial threats of 787–8, following a serious conspiracy in 785–6 – and what we can safely take to have been inspired by these, just as the capitulary of Herstal had been inspired by the crisis of 778 (p. 13), his second great reform capitulary, the *General Admonition* of 789. Much emphasis is laid in this lengthy and highly important document on clerical obedience to the canons; most of its articles, in fact, are based upon texts contained in the canon law collection known as the *Dionysio-Hadriana* which Charles had brought back from Italy in 774. But the capitulary goes a great deal wider and deeper than that, amounting to a statement of the Christian principles – peace, concord, equity and so forth – upon which the social transformation referred to above (p. 14) is to be based. As this capitulary reflected Charles's piety and zeal, so did the campaign against the pagan Avars, which was certainly seen as a holy war. For three days in early September, encamped on the Enns river-frontier, the king's army devoted itself to litanies and masses, alms-giving and psalm-singing. Other armies march on their stomachs; Charles's fasted, to gain spiritual sustenance. No one can read Charles's letter to his wife Fastrada giving details of the efforts to enlist God's aid in the travails ahead and asking for similar action at home and remain unconvinced of the strength and sincerity of his piety. The letter, disconcertingly conventional in its personal features – Charles sends loving greetings to wife and darling daughters; he is safe and sound; he is surprised not to have had a letter since Regensburg – tells us that a force from Italy had already attacked and heavily defeated the Avars in late August. Consequent demoralization was perhaps one reason why they did not stand and fight when Charles advanced into their territory, ships on the Danube and an army on each bank, but fled their fortified positions. Resistance was minimal, and the king reached the Rába before turning back with immense spoils and numbers of captives. The triumph was marred only by the loss of almost all the thousands of horses to a pestilence.

Probably this explains the lack of an Avar campaign in 792. Charles stayed in Bavaria, doubtless supervising the extension of Frankish control over the region, between the Enns and, roughly, Vienna, which alone was incorporated into the kingdom, and planned a major attack for 793. He evidently saw the Avars as still a formidable force, as did the Saxons and Saracens (pp. 23, 45). However, the offensive had to be cancelled, and the king played no further direct role in the Pannonian theatre. He was not needed, for the Avar 'state' fell apart. Civil wars brought the deaths of the two supreme chieftains, the khagan and the jugur, who were doubtless blamed for the failure in 791, and in 795–6 another potentate, the tudun, appeared at Aachen with a large following to submit himself and his people to Charles and to undergo baptism. We hear of no opposition to the troops sent by Eric, duke of Friuli, who in 795, in an exploit much impressing Alcuin, entered the ring, the great earthwork somewhere between the Danube and the Tisza which served as the khagans' seat, and plundered it of some of the treasure amassed there over the generations. Eric sent this to Charles who, as a true king and lord, distributed it widely among churches and his *fideles*; much went to Rome and some to Offa of Mercia and, probably, other rulers. In 796, while some Avars fled across the Tisza, the new khagan submitted to Pippin, who then had his army destroy the ring and remove the remaining treasure, also destined for Charles. Booty-taking was a direct objective, not just an incidental benefit of contemporary campaigning; hence the constancy with which the sources refer to it. But no war in memory, declared Einhard, so enriched the Franks as that against the Avars.

Perhaps it was this consideration which led Einhard to call the Avar war the most important Charles fought except for that against the Saxons. Militarily, it seems hardly to merit the name of war after 791; and even then, as we saw, Charles's expedition was something of a promenade. There were Avar troubles in 797, 798–9 (when Gerold of Bavaria was killed) and 802–3, but the very fact that we hear little about these suggests that they were not so very serious. Indeed, the Avars soon needed Charles's protection against the neighbouring Slavs (p. 47). Had the Franks extended direct control beyond the region indicated above, greater problems might have arisen. As it was, the easterly areas, though subject to Charles, remained under native princely authority. Despite the interest of Alcuin (who, with Saxony in mind, insisted that conversion must be by persuasion, not force) and others, there was no significant missionary activity. It was into the vacuum of this eastern marcher territory that another Asiatic people would move late in the ninth century, to become no less a scourge to western Europe than the Avars had been to eastern: the Magyars.

SAXONY, 792–804

What forced the cancellation of the Avar campaign planned for 793 was a major reverse on the Weser, where Saxons had attacked and destroyed a body of troops bound for Pannonia. Saxony had seemed pacified. Nothing indicates difficulties there between 786 and 791, a period offering several instances of Saxon participation in campaigns and attendance at assemblies. But a limited rebellion, incited by expectation of Avar vengeance on the Franks and inspired by loyalty to paganism, had broken out there already in 792; churches had been burned, clerics killed. Slavs and Frisians had also revolted, and the Saxon rebels had sent emissaries to the Avars. It was no doubt in anticipation of the problems of a two-front war that Charles, rather than respond immediately to the Weser disaster, devoted the autumn of 793 to the attempted construction of a navigable channel between the rivers Altmühl and Rednitz, tributaries respectively of the Danube and the Main (which itself joins the Rhine). This extraordinary enterprise, involving a labour-force of many thousands drawn from a wide area and the numerous attendant problems of transportation, provisioning and so forth, provides striking testimony to the reality of the king's power of command. The benefits of success would have been great, and not only logistic. But for all the skill of the surveyors and engineers, local geology defeated the project, as it did also in Napoleon's day.

The work was still in progress when news came that the Saxon troubles had escalated into general revolt. One might conjecture that a contributory factor was economic distress, caused by a combination of famine and the burden of tithe. Famine struck the Frankish kingdom following harvest-failure in 792 and was both widespread and exceptionally cruel. Characteristically, Charles responded with religious measures; but he also commanded that practical aid be given and fixed maximum prices for corn. As for tithe, Alcuin leaves no doubt of the seriousness of this as a Saxon grievance in the mid-790s; its obligations would have weighed all the heavier during dearth.

Not until autumn 794, after the synod of Frankfurt (p. 36), did the king take action. But it had satisfying results, for the rebels surrendered without a fight when two armies, under Charles and his namesake son, converged on them near Paderborn. The king's benevolence in freeing the captives after they had simply renewed their oaths might be explained by pity if they were indeed in economic distress; alternatively, he may have calculated that generosity would be most likely to win their loyalty. But the Saxons failed to join him for the intended campaign of 795, and it was against them, therefore, that this came to be directed. Those yielding peacefully joined the king, who ravaged the more ferociously on hearing that the Nordliudi had killed his vassal, the Abodrite king, as he advanced to give support. Finally, all the rebels save the North Saxons submitted; their lives were spared as promised, but Charles took droves of hostages, every third man according to one source, 7070 in another. While resistance perhaps flickered on into 797, it is 795 which marks the effective end of the long struggle with the South Saxons. Westphalians, Eastphalians and Angrarians all participated in the Aachen council which, in October 797, agreed the measures incorporated in a second Saxon capitulary. Often compared most favourably with the first (p. 16), it actually covers distinct ground save in a couple of cases where, it is true, penalties are softened. Nothing suggests a general annulment of the earlier rulings, including that on tithe. Nevertheless, the tone is certainly more moderate. Charles and his army stayed in Saxony for the winter. But the southern troubles were finally over.

By contrast, the subjection of the northerners, previously almost unmentioned in the sources, was only just beginning. In both 796 and 797 Charles was in Wihmodia, the region between the lower Weser and the lower Elbe, wasting, burning and taking numerous captives, in whose place Franks were settled. Submission resulted, but in 798 the Wihmodians were again in rebellion, as were the Nordliudi across the Elbe, who killed royal legates and also an ambassador returning from Denmark. Against these latter Charles used the vengeful Abodrites, who defeated them, killing almost 3000; the survivors submitted, giving hostages. The king himself harried Wihmodia: 1600 leading men were taken as hostages. In 799 there were mass deportations, the vacated lands being bestowed upon the king's *fideles*, lay and clerical. Evidently resistance continued, for an army (of Saxons!) was wasting north of the Elbe in 802. Two years later the depopulation policy initiated in 795 was taken to its drastic extreme when Charles himself supervised the army's deportation of the entire population of Wihmodia and the lands across the Elbe, which last he granted to the Abodrites. Einhard reports 10,000 male deportees alone. No solution could have been more final.

In talking of a thirty-three-year war with the Saxons Einhard misleads. In at least ten years between 772 and 804 fighting is both un-evidenced and most unlikely. Moreover, there was really a series of separate wars with different groups of Saxons – if 'war' is the appropriate term to describe hostilities which were usually between a king and rebellious subjects. Nevertheless, the struggle with the Saxons unquestionably constitutes the reign's major military theme. It is also of the very highest historical significance. Quite simply, without Charles's incorporation of Saxony into the Frankish kingdom the emergence of Germany as a political entity would be inconceivable.

No account of the first half of Charles's reign can fail to accord the central position to campaigning. The king's successes were of permanent significance, determining the shape of French, Italian and German history down to this very day. But there are other matters which require discussion, both for their intrinsic importance and because they aid understanding of the theme upon which historical attention naturally, and rightly, comes to focus in the 790s, that of emperorship. To these we now turn.

Charles, Rome and Constantinople, 768–88

CHARLES AND THE PAPACY, 768–81

Remarks above about western reverence for Rome and Charles's own piety might suggest that he was the obedient servant of the papal will. Not at all. Wholly in the tradition of western political thought, but the more firmly for his strong religious sense, he regarded himself as the appointee of God, Who granted him power for the benefit of the subjects divinely entrusted to his care and to Whom he must answer – fearsome prospect! – for the discharge of his ministry. There could be no question of abdicating his responsibilities, and perhaps of imperilling his immortal soul, by allowing decisions affecting the health of the society committed to his charge to rest elsewhere. The absence of any contemporary conception of 'church' and 'state' as distinct, autonomous institutions must be stressed; when Charles appointed bishops, laid down priestly duties, ruled on monastic life and so on he was simply directing the authority he held over the whole of Christian society towards one of the two groups of people making it up, the clergy as opposed to the laity. The popes did not challenge this authority. But they did make many demands upon Charles, speaking in the name of St Peter and emphasizing both his status as holder of the keys of the heavenly kingdom and the immensity of the earthly and heavenly rewards which stood to be gained by pleasing him. Charles revered the saint, was generally respectful to the popes, particularly Hadrian, for whom he developed a genuine affection, and saw it as his duty to protect them. But he none the less followed his own judgement, which often enough ran counter to theirs.

Charles's attitude was displayed already in 770, when he disregarded Stephen's threat of excommunication (p. 7). But he did respond to Hadrian's request for help against Desiderius (p. 10) and at Easter 774 paid the first of four visits to Rome. He came unannounced, and Hadrian, though having him greeted with the honours befitting a patrician, was clearly wary; only after a reciprocal oath was Charles

26

permitted to enter the city. Before he left Hadrian's reservations will have vanished, for the outcome of the visit was a deed of donation whereby Charles seemingly granted vast tracts of Italy to St Peter. This document, modelled on Pippin's donation of 754 (p. 5) and subscribed and sworn to by the king and leading Franks in St Peter's (where a copy was left on the saint's body), is known as the Donation of Charlemagne, and great is the controversy which it has spawned. It does not survive and the only direct guide to its contents appears in a problematic passage of Hadrian's biography. Some historians have judged this a forger's later insertion. How could Charles conceivably have sworn to hand over such extensive territories, including Spoleto, Benevento and the imperial provinces of Istria and Venetia? And why, if he did so swear, did he not, pious ruler and enemy of the perjurer that he was, implement his promises in so far as he could?

There are no easy answers to these questions, but the 'forgery' thesis is nowadays generally rejected. Without doubt there *was* a donation; Hadrian's earlier letters after 774 frequently urge Charles to implement it in full, show that in his view it embraced Spoleto and the (previously papal) north-eastern regions of Ravenna, Emilia and Pentapolis, and do not preclude a wider scope. It may be that the solution lies not so much in what the *Life of Hadrian* says as in what it does not. There may have been conditions, for example; or the gift may have been based on an inaccurate understanding of circumstances; or the donation may have drawn a distinction not reproduced in the *Life* between patrimonies within territories and territories themselves, that is, between private land rights and public governmental ones. Consensus on this matter is the remotest of prospects.

After Charles's assumption of the Lombard kingship, Hadrian had difficulty even in reasserting authority over lands seized by Desiderius, for archbishop Leo of Ravenna, claiming his own grant from Charles, occupied certain cities and held them, probably, until his death in 777. If Charles did not intervene here, despite Hadrian's appeals and denunciations of Leo, nor did he hand over Spoleto. The Spoletans had, in fact, already given allegiance to St Peter in autumn 773; but by January 776 at the latest Hildebrand, the duke appointed by Hadrian himself, had acknowledged Charles's lordship. The king's planned visit to Rome in autumn 775, during which Hadrian was expecting the fulfilment of the donation, did not materialize; worse, the envoys he sent in his place went to Spoleto – which, the angry pope reminded Charles, he had given to St Peter – and then to Benevento before presenting themselves at Rome to ask Hadrian to forgive Hildebrand his offence, that is, presumably, his breach of fidelity.

Hadrian's letter of early 776 to Charles, reporting this request, goes on to tell of his discovery of a plot against pope and king. Allegedly, the dukes of Benevento, Spoleto, Friuli and Chiusi – the first three of whom the pope had frequently previously denounced as conspirators – were to combine with a Greek force in March 776 in order to seize Rome, take the pope captive and restore Adelchis to the Lombard throne. Adelchis was Desiderius's son and co-king who had fled to Constantinople. The common judgement that this conspiracy was Hadrian's invention seems wilful. In fact, Rodgaud of Friuli had already rebelled in late 775, to be met by an immediate response from Charles, who marched into Italy early in the new year, disposed of him and recaptured the revolted cities. His swiftness of action is sufficient to explain the conspiracy's abortion, though the death of the emperor Constantine V in September 775 would probably have put paid to it in any case.

Charles did not go to Rome in 776; and a planned visit in 778 fell through (p. 12). Disappointed, Hadrian wrote a celebrated letter (p. 35) in which, though still urging full implementation of the donation, he also requested the restoration of patrimonies belonging to the papacy (documentary proof had already been forwarded) but seized from it over the years. Hadrian had evidently concluded that an extension of papal public authority in Italy was unlikely and that concentration on private land rights might be more fruitful. Shortly afterwards, responding to Beneventan intrigues with the Byzantine governor of Sicily and the city of Terracina, within the nominally Byzantine duchy of Naples, to incite his subjects' defection, Hadrian mounted the first offensive military campaign in papal history and subjected Terracina 'to the service of St Peter, yourself and ourself', as he put it to the king. The city was soon recaptured by the Neapolitans, who had Greek and Beneventan support, and Hadrian appealed for Charles's aid. Supposedly duke Arichis of Benevento was in constant contact with the governor of Sicily and only awaiting Adelchis's arrival to attack the pope and, through him, the king. Hadrian achieved neither of his objectives in this episode: to regain lost southern patrimonies (for which he was willing to barter Terracina) or to involve Charles in the region, doubtless with a view to papal advantage. But there is no reason to think the Byzantine–Beneventan collusion he reports fictitious. Indeed, it may have been precisely to placate a protesting Charles that in February 781 the imperial government sent a new governor to Sicily.

For by this time Constantinople was seeking a Frankish marriage alliance. The initiative is often connected with a change of imperial religious policy. Despite western denunciation, iconoclasm (p. 5) had remained the eastern orthodoxy under the emperor Constantine V (741–75). But already, in the reign of Leo IV (775–80) there were signs that the iconoclast tide was turning; and under the formidable Irene, a woman profoundly devoted to image-veneration, who became regent for her ten-year-old son Constantine VI on her husband's death in September 780, it soon found itself in full ebb. By 784 Irene felt ready to proceed to iconoclasm's formal overthrow by a great council. Although its first meeting, in 786, was broken up by hostile soldiers, it reconvened at Nicaea in autumn 787, with papal legates participating, and duly pronounced for the orthodoxy of image-veneration. Doctrinal union with Rome had been restored. Despite Hadrian's demands, however, the rights and patrimonies lost under Leo III (p. 5) had not.

It is difficult to see why anti-iconoclasm should be thought the spur to the marriage enterprise of 781, however. It had evidently not been what prompted Constantine V to make a comparable proposal to Pippin III. Moreover, factors of time and distance suggest Leo IV rather than Irene as the initiator. Probably the Byzantine concern was, first, to protect the empire's western territories, the fate of which mattered more to its rulers than many historians care to believe, and, second, to gain an ally who might act against any threat arising to the government from those regions. For Charles, alliance would bring such tangible political advantages as the removal of Adelchis's threat and greater security in southern Italy. But prestige will have mattered greatly; it is easily forgotten that Carolingian kingship was only thirty years old and Charles of noble, not royal, birth.

The betrothal itself, involving Constantine and the little Rotrud, was concluded between Charles and imperial ambassadors at Rome at Easter 781. Irene's intentions towards iconoclasm will have been spelled out; Charles would not have had his daughter marry a schismatic. And it is very likely that Constantinople now recognized the *status quo* in Italy. General considerations support this hypothesis, and Hadrian's substitution of papal for imperial years for dating purposes (first witnessed in 781, though not necessarily belonging then) and the issue of an independent coinage may have been in consequence. Besides other events (pp. 10, 19), Charles's 781 visit also saw a territorial agreement with

29

Hadrian, who was confirmed in possession of the lands he already held, granted Sabina, near Rome (which the Spoletans proved reluctant to hand over, despite royal *missi*), and allotted certain financial rights, apparently in lieu of his Tuscan and other Spoletan claims.

When Charles next came to Rome, in 787, it was *en route* to the duchy of Benevento, which he had resolved to subject. The king had demonstrated in 783 that the Beneventans should take the allegiance they owed seriously by having the abbot of S. Vincenzo arrested and tried for disloyalty. But Benevento's remoteness gave duke Arichis – who called himself 'prince' – great freedom. It was perhaps his attack on Byzantine Amalfi in 786 which occasioned Charles's offensive; the king was an imperial ally. Urged by Hadrian and the leading Franks to ignore Arichis's protestations of obedience, Charles advanced to Capua, and Arichis responded by retreating to the heavily fortified Salerno. Perhaps Charles genuinely wished to avoid the devastation of the land, as the annalist states; but perhaps he thought better of exposing his troops to the diseases and other hazards of a lengthy southern campaign. In any case, he withdrew after taking hostages, receiving fresh oaths of loyalty and obliging the duke to payment of tribute. Arichis should have paid a territorial price also, for Charles granted Hadrian Capua and other cities in the duchy as well as the old papal patrimonies there. But the pope never acquired these, unlike Tuscan cities, including Viterbo and Orvieto, conferred at the same time.

Charles had a further purpose in visiting Italy in 787: to confer with imperial ambassadors. The meeting took place in Capua, and the envoys, who had come to fetch Rotrud, went away empty-handed. Historians have usually regarded her non-delivery as tantamount to Charles's annulment of the betrothal and hence of the alliance. No source, in fact, suggests this. He may well have insisted on waiting until iconoclasm had been renounced. Charles had ambassadors in the east in the mid-780s and other sources of information; he knew the situation. The common attribution of his alleged decision to outrage at Irene's failure to invite him or any of his clerics to the anti-iconoclast council is wholly speculative. Outrage is somewhat difficult to swallow, given that the invitations had gone out back in 785. According to Theophanes, a contemporary Byzantine chronicler, it was Irene who broke off the betrothal, and this not until 788. No sound reason exists to reject this evidence. And the date shows that her decision was not in immediate response to the non-delivery of Rotrud.

It was, rather, territorial ambition which prompted her. No sooner had Charles left Capua than Arichis had sent legates declaring his readiness, in return for the duchy of Naples and military aid, to accept imperial sovereignty. Benevento was an alluring prize, and Arichis's offer opened grander vistas yet. When Irene's envoys left Constantinople to confer the patriciate on Arichis as he had asked they took the message that Adelchis – his brother-in-law, whose presence he had also requested – would be dispatched to Treviso or Ravenna with an army. Irene, in other words, her hands now freed by the religious peace, was thinking in terms of northern Italian conquest. It is well on the cards that Bavarian and Avar support was also arranged (p. 21).

In the event the legates arrived, in January 788, to find both Arichis and his elder son dead. But they were assured by his widow Adelperga and the Beneventan leaders that Charles had been asked to appoint Grimoald, Arichis's younger son, a hostage with the king, as duke and that he would carry out his father's commitments. Papal letters and a report from one of the royal *missi* sent to Benevento alerted Charles to the disloyalty which was rife there and which even involved plots to seize or kill the *missi*; and Hadrian, disclosing the intrigues with the Byzantines, entreated him not to appoint Grimoald. Charles, no doubt already aware of Tassilo's disloyalty, was faced with an acute dilemma but eventually, in May 788, after Adelchis had already landed, installed Grimoald. Presumably he calculated that Grimoald might remain loyal, whereas an adverse decision would inevitably set the resentful Beneventans against him. The gamble succeeded. When the imperial attack came, late in 788, the Beneventans under Grimoald stood alongside the Spoletans under Hildebrand and a Frankish force under Winigis – Hildebrand's successor in 789 – to defeat it in Calabria. The battle was a major affair: the reviser reports an 'immense multitude' of the enemy killed and a 'great number' captured, and a letter, offering a rare control, gives content to these imprecise phrases in mentioning 4000 imperial dead and 1000 prisoners.

Although the war begun in 788 came to a formal end only after Charles's death, imperial forces were not again engaged in the west until 806 (p. 44), despite Charles's occupation of Istria early on. But two offensives by Pippin against Beneventan territory in the early 790s were almost certainly directed at an imperial ally. For Grimoald swiftly broke the terms of his appointment, and the fact that he not only married Constantine's sister-in-law but also repudiated her after Constantine's repudiation of her sister in 795 very strongly suggests that he stood with the Byzantines. He was to be attacked again (p. 40).

31

The breach with Irene was of far greater moment than the scant military consequences would indicate, however. For it was the precondition of a theological and ideological offensive against Constantinople which may fairly be seen as the beginning of a road ending with Charles's assumption of emperorship in 800.

The coronation of 800

THE *Libri Carolini* AND THE CAROLINGIAN RENAISSANCE

The immediate target of this offensive was the council of Nicaea (p. 29). Its decrees were known only through a woeful translation sent from Rome; in particular, where the Greek spoke of the 'veneration' of images, carefully distinguishing this from 'worship', due to God alone, the Latin had 'adoration'. The errors made denunciation easier, but the attack was by no means dependent upon them. It was mounted in a lengthy work probably completed in 792 and usually known as the *Libri Carolini* ('Caroline Books'). Its author was probably Theodulf, later bishop of Orléans, but it was written in Charles's name and he was certainly involved in its composition. Trenchant, scornful, sometimes vituperative, it assailed both the council of 787 and an earlier iconoclast council of 754 with a battery of learned arguments, maintaining that images must be neither destroyed nor adored nor venerated; their role was to decorate and to instruct. It also examined other matters, theological and ideological. Particularly significant are its denunciations of the manifestations of the so-called imperial cult and the contrast it drew between the arrogance of Irene and Constantine, who called themselves 'divine', and the humility of the king, who held himself God's servant and his office a ministry for the doing of His will. Although asserting Roman primacy in matters of faith (and although Frankish clerics had declared for image-veneration in a Roman council of 769), the *Libri* patently denied it by their theological standpoint. Hadrian, sent an early draft, defended Nicaea (while also offering to excommunicate Constantine should he fail to meet the pope's other demands), but Charles was unmoved. When, in 794, papal legates at the synod of Frankfurt (p. 36) accepted its condemnation of Nicaea, Hadrian had sacrificed integrity to expedience. There, however, the issue was allowed tacitly to rest.

This is an appropriate moment to comment briefly on the Carolingian Renaissance, as the burgeoning of intellectual life under Charles has been dubbed, for the *Libri* testify to the advanced, self-confident character of scholarship north of the Alps. We may be sure that, though written by a single hand, the work was collaborative in as much as it was the product of the interplay of many able minds, intensive debate and testing criticism. Francia under Charles knew an unprecedented ferment of scholarly activity, and for this the king himself was chiefly responsible. His own enthusiasm for and pursuit of learning is particularly evident from Einhard and the letters of the Anglo-Saxon Alcuin, the most renowned of the cosmopolitan band of scholars he gathered around him. And he promoted education. A late eighth-century capitulary, *On Cultivating Letters*, announced that bishoprics and monasteries should undertake the task of teaching 'those who by the Lord's gift are able to learn'; the *General Admonition* of 789 (p. 21) ordered every monastery and see to provide schools; and there are further indications, including a directive of 802 from Theodulf of Orléans that his priests should open free local schools. We should beware of exaggerating the material legacy: injunction is one thing, implementation another; moreover, a destructive age lay not far ahead. Nevertheless, it was upon the foundation of Charles's educational achievement that the imposing intellectual edifice of the central middle ages was raised. No less important, Charles's reputation ensured an enduring association between good rulership and the fostering of intellectual life, to Europe's immeasurable benefit.

Why this fostering? Essentially, because Charles was intent upon the reshaping of society in accordance with the tenets of Christianity (p. 14) and because the prerequisite to attainment of this objective was knowledge. As *On Cultivating Letters* put it: 'For although it is better to do what is good than to know it, yet knowing comes before doing.' There is no question of an orchestration of the scholarly work of the age. Even the old view that Charles sought to establish an 'authorized' biblical text has now been discarded. Rather, educated men responded to a climate of ideological reform in which they were indispensable figures because they alone could unlock the Christian knowledge which was reform's necessary foundation. The role within the society of Charles's day of the monks who laboured to copy the repositories of Christian truth and the scholars who wrote to interpret this or to expound its practical consequences may perfectly properly be compared with that of the publishers, commentators and so forth of the works of Marx and Lenin in twentieth-century Soviet society.

The prime such repository was, of course, the Bible, which was regarded as God's textbook for man's guidance, not just in the moral and spiritual spheres but in all his multifarious concerns, private and public. Everything was there for the man who looked with the eyes of faith – and knowledge. Hence the abundance of bibles; according to the late Walter Ullmann, 'in relative terms, at no other time in European history was the Bible so frequently copied in so short a time' as in the last two decades of the reign. Hence, too, the scholarly concern with correct Latin, for the literal word of God must not be sullied by error or be misunderstood. But there were numerous other sources of Christian knowledge and guides to Christian life: works of the fathers, like Augustine's *City of God*, Charles's own favourite; canon law collections, like the *Dionysio-Hadriana* (p. 22); the monastic Rule of St Benedict, which he acquired from Monte Cassino itself in 787; and so forth.

There is a lot more to the Carolingian Renaissance, barely touched on here, than is embraced by the above interpretation, which is essentially Ullmann's. But nothing better represents its essence.

THE EXALTATION OF CHARLEMAGNE

It is in the early 790s that we encounter the first signs of what may be termed an imperialization of Charles. Without doubt the development was precipitated by the dispute with Constantinople. The ideological scrutiny in which the *Libri Carolini* engaged both revealed the impropriety of emperorship as practised in the east and confirmed Charles's own notions of what it meant to be a true Christian monarch. The combination looks to have had a potent psychological impact, heightening his self-confidence, removing any lingering suspicion that the ruler in Constantinople held a superior authority, leading him, indeed, to feel that ruler his inferior. The exalted self-conception with which Charles emerged is demonstrated in his very authorization of the *Libri*, a work censuring and denigrating the ruler traditionally viewed as the highest lay dignitary of Christendom, denouncing the doctrinal judgement of an imperially and papally sanctioned council of the church and asserting an opposed position in defiance of papal remonstrance. Like any emperor, Charles was acting as the guardian of true doctrine. There is a manifestly imperial ring, moreover, to his designation in the *Libri* as 'by the will of God king of the Franks, ruling with the Lord's aid over the Gauls, Germany, Italy and their adjacent provinces'.

Incipient imperial sentiment found concrete expression in the new palace complex constructed at Aachen. Work seems to have begun about 790 and enough had been done by 794 for Charles to celebrate

Christmas in what became his almost invariable winter residence. Debate has raged about the architectural inspiration, especially of the chapel, but the arguments are too technical to permit even summary here. In any case, the possibility of an imperial model is less important than the fact that Aachen was built as a fixed capital for Charles – just as Constantinople (infinitely grander, of course) had been for the emperor Constantine 450 years before. Indeed, just as the great eastern metropolis was termed 'Second Rome' so, in a poem of 799 (p. 37), was Aachen.

Northern sources do not liken Charles to Constantine, however, even though their common services to the faith made the comparison natural. This may be because the Constantine of the late eighth century was the Constantine of the Donation (p. 5) and comparison would have borne embarrassing implications. Hadrian had shown why in a letter of 778 urging Charles to fulfil his donation and exalt the Roman church as Constantine had done 'that all peoples who hear of this may be able to proclaim: "Lord, save the king; and hear us when we call upon Thee; for behold, a new Constantine, God's most Christian emperor, has arisen in these times, through whom God has vouchsafed to bestow all things upon His holy church of St Peter"'. The passage is celebrated, but the approach lacked finesse and Hadrian had no further recourse to Constantine. Very late in the 790s, however, he was again linked with Charles by pope Leo III (795–816), in a Lateran mosaic which showed, on the one hand, Christ presenting the keys to St Peter and a standard to Constantine, on the other, Peter handing a pallium to Leo and, again, a standard to Charles. The possible implications cannot be explored here, but the fact of a parallel is manifest.

It was, rather, to warn Charles against following Constantine's lapse into heresy that archbishop Elipand of (Muslim) Toledo referred to the emperor in a letter of 792. Elipand and Felix of Urgel (in Frankish Spain) were the leading exponents of Adoptianism, a doctrine currently widespread in Spain which maintained that Christ, in His human nature, was the adoptive, not the true, Son of God. Adoptianism's interest for us lies in Charles's response: the king had Felix brought to Regensburg in 792 and his teachings condemned as heresy by a synod of bishops. So might an emperor have acted. The papal condemnation which followed when Felix was taken to Rome to repeat his retraction was no more than a confirmation. Throughout the dispute – which continued, for Felix soon relapsed – all concerned saw Charles as the decision-maker.

35

Adoptianism was first on the agenda at the synod of Frankfurt in 794. It is evident that Charles intended this great assembly as the west's counterblast to Nicaea. Papal legates attended, as did clerics from all parts of his dominions and even beyond, together with laymen. The capitulary containing Frankfurt's rulings is the third great reform capitulary of the reign, after Herstal and the *General Admonition*, and as these both followed bad times, so did Frankfurt: 792–3 had seen conspiracy, famine, Avar alarms, Saxon rebellion and Saracen attack (pp. 8, 22–4, 45). Most of the rulings are concerned with canon law, monastic life and the like, though Tassilo was also dealt with (p. 20) and there were important socio-economic measures. But at the head of the capitulary stands the denunciation of Adoptianism; second comes the rejection of the 787 council's alleged decision on images, grossly misrepresented as ruling that they should be adored like the Trinity. The contrast is pointed and the message clear: the west has its own heresy, a serious matter, but stands united and orthodox under Charles in condemning it; compare the east! It can hardly be doubted that Charles, who opened and closed the debates, was deliberately presenting himself at Frankfurt as *de facto* emperor of the west.

Important also is further Roman evidence. When, in late 795, Leo III notified Charles of his election he also sent him the standard of the city of Rome and asked that an envoy come to receive oaths of loyalty from its people. Since a standard was a customary symbol of secular authority, it looks very much as if Leo was bestowing this upon the king in Rome and that the oath was that required from all the king's subjects since 789. If so, the portrayal of Charles in Leo's mosaic was perhaps functionally equivalent to the imperial portraits earlier displayed in Rome in token of the absent rulers' authority – the difference being that in the mosaic Leo also appeared. This might indicate co-rulership, suggested also by Leo's practice, from 798, of dating documents by both papal years and the years of Charles's possession of Italy. But whether or not Charles held (or was considered by Leo to hold) a degree of authority in the old imperial capital before 800, he certainly expressed himself with imperial authoritativeness in instructing Leo to comport himself correctly and pronouncing upon their respective functions: his to defend the church by arms and to strengthen it internally in knowledge of the faith, Leo's to pray.

Given space, further features would repay scrutiny: imitation of Byzantine chancery practices; relations with other rulers, including the caliph and the Asturian king; increasing employment of imperial epithets like 'orthodox'; Charles's frequent denomination as David 'as though to express the divine repudiation of the new Saul [the emperor]' (Robert Folz); and the use, especially by Alcuin, of *imperium* to designate Charles's dominions (a usage less decisive than may appear since *imperium* meant 'realm' as well as the normal 'empire').

The evidence is cumulatively irresistible: the 790s saw the recasting of Charles in an imperial mould. It is scarcely conceivable that the possibility of his assuming the imperial title itself had not been mooted well before their end. Especially so, since from August 797, when she had her son disqualified as emperor by blinding, Irene ruled in her own right. A woman's emperorship was unprecedented; it might also be deemed invalid. So it was, at Rome in 800.

THE CORONATION OF 800

Few historical events, if any, have been the subject of more exhaustive investigation and controversy than Charles's elevation to emperorship on Christmas Day 800. It is impossible even to indicate here, let alone to grapple with, the various theses, so numerous are they. What follows, therefore, will not be a balanced exploration of the points at issue and the interpretations they have evoked but a necessarily somewhat dogmatic statement of the author's judgement on a very limited number of the questions which the event raises.

On 25 April 799, as he rode through Rome, Leo fell victim to a pre-arranged attack led by two important papal officers, one a nephew of Hadrian. There are earlier signs of hostility, and many nobles were implicated in the plot. But political motivation is not evidenced and there may be no deeper explanation than outrage at Leo's impropriety of life, which can be taken as certain. For reasons not easily divined, attempts to put out Leo's eyes and cut out his tongue – such mutilation would have disqualified him from office – failed. (It was widely believed, however, that they had succeeded and that a miracle restored his faculties.) Imprisoned, the pope was secretly rescued, taken by duke Winigis to Spoleto and from there escorted north to join Charles in July at Paderborn – for the king, whose first inclination had been to go to Rome, had eventually decided to proceed with his planned Saxon expedition.

A fascinating contemporary poem by a court *littérateur*, the *Paderborn Epic*, tells of Leo's reception and reveals a markedly imperial conception of Charles: Aachen is 'Rome of the future'; the king is 'father of Europe', its 'summit', its 'beacon', 'head of the world', 'David', even 'Augustus'. The situation no doubt contributed powerfully to the advance of such imperializing sentiments, which find loftier expression in a letter of Alcuin in June 799: Charles is one of the three highest persons in the world: the pope's fate is known; the emperor has been deposed; it is upon him alone, 'the governor of the Christian people' by Christ's dispensation and surpassing the others in power, wisdom and dignity, that the church's salvation entirely depends.

Charges of simony, perjury and fornication which followed Leo to Paderborn caused disquiet; some felt he should not be restored. But restoration, we may think, was a foregone conclusion. The real problem was how to lay the charges to rest. Canon law forbade judgement of a pope, as Alcuin pointed out. Even to require an oath of innocence, as some suggested, would be, in a fashion, to judge. The solution eventually adopted, a (theoretically) voluntary oath of innocence, will certainly have been agreed before Leo left Paderborn in October, to be escorted back to Rome by royal *missi*. These arrested the leading conspirators after a brief enquiry and sent them to the king, who took them back to Rome in 800. Evidently Charles already held, or was prepared to exercise, jurisdiction over Romans, and there is no reason to think, despite a celebrated thesis by Heldmann maintaining his elevation to emperorship to have been necessary to establish a supreme judicial authority in Rome, that because he judged these men after it he could not as well have done so before.

According to a source of about a century later, *The Deeds of the Bishops of Naples*, Paderborn saw another decision: Leo promised to crown Charles with the imperial diadem. There is, in fact, a very powerful circumstantial case for believing that Charles's elevation to emperorship was agreed already at Paderborn. First, the king waited over a year before going to Rome. That nothing compelling detained him is apparent from the entries in the annals for early 800: one reports that he went on progress, another that he toured his estates and saints' burial-places, a third that he went fishing! We know that he visited Angilbert in St-Riquier, Alcuin in Tours and Theodulf in Orléans, all trusted figures, and that all his sons were with him in Tours. There was more substantial business, true: he created a Channel fleet against Scandinavian pirates, organized coastal defences and received the formal submission of the Bretons, subjected in 799 by count Wido. Even so, the impression that he was killing time while also composing himself for what lay ahead is irresistible. If Paderborn had seen agreement on elevation to emperorship, it would surely have seen it also on the theatrical timing: what day was more fitting for Charles's imperial 'rebirth' than Christ's own birthday (Charles had always previously visited Rome at Easter), what year more appropriate than the nativity's centennial, what combination better calculated than the great festival and the opening year of a new century to make the maximum impact upon contemporaries and posterity? Alcuin knew of the arrangement, to judge by the wholly fitting gift he sent for presentation to 'David' on Christmas Day 'for the splendour of your imperial power' – the revised Bible to which he had been devoting all his time earlier in 800 – and by the imperial phraseology of the accompanying letter.

Second, when Charles arrived outside Rome on 23 November he was met twelve miles from the city by Leo. Formerly, an exarch had been received at the first milestone (like Charles in 774), an emperor – who alone merited personal papal reception – at the sixth. The honour paid Charles was, so to speak, supra-imperial. It was also public. The implications are obvious.

Significant, third is the evidence of the *Lorsch Annals* that Charles agreed publicly shortly before Christmas to accept the name of emperor. A week after arriving he opened a council in St Peter's to examine the matter of the charges against the pope. Leo's accusers appeared, but the king held them motivated by malice; moreover, no one was willing to judge the pope. On 23 December, therefore, Leo mounted the pulpit, gospels in hand, and swore his oath. It was after this that the assembly – of Romans and Franks, laymen and clerics – asked Charles to take the name of emperor, a petition to which he 'with all humility' assented. Plainly he will have known of the proposal beforehand. But it is at the least unlikely that it had been put only after his arrival. Four weeks would scarcely have sufficed for due consideration of the matter, especially of the consequences *vis-à-vis* Constantinople. For the *Lorsch Annals* give the grounds for the assembly's request: first, 'the name of emperor was lacking among the Greeks . . . they had female rule'; second, Charles possessed, by God's grant, Rome, 'where the Caesars had always been accustomed to have their seat' and the rest of the imperial residences 'throughout Italy, Gaul and Germany'. Self-evidently, it was as successor to Constantine VI, as latest in a line of rulers stretching back to Augustus, that Charles was envisaged. In as much as western lands would now be ruled again by an emperor, there would be a restoration of the empire: here is one reason for the device which would appear on his imperial seal: 'renewal of the

Roman empire'. But by taking the name of emperor Charles would automatically be asserting a right to rule the existing empire – the Byzantine lands, that is – for although there were many precedents for simultaneous government by two emperors within the single empire, in the assembly's judgement no emperor existed in the east. In practice, however, Irene held sway. Problems were inevitable.

And, fourth, there are possible indications that Charles had taken measures in anticipation of these. One might speculate that the otherwise unexplained dispatch of a legate to Paderborn by the governor of Sicily was in response to soundings as to his future attitude. The nominally imperial Balearic islands did in fact transfer their allegiance to Charles in 799. While the arrival of a legate from the patriarch of Jerusalem late in 799 was certainly fortuitous, it asks too much to suppose that the envoy whom the king then sent east should have appeared back in Rome, with patriarchal legates bearing the keys of the Holy Places and the keys and banner of Jerusalem, on 23 December 800 itself, by sheer coincidence. Rather, this looks like careful stage-management to maximize the propaganda impact of a declaration for Charles by the Christian leader of the east's – indeed, the faith's – holiest city (albeit one under caliphal rule). Again, when Charles went to Italy he had Pippin mount a campaign against Benevento, renewing this in 801–2. Not only was Benevento almost certainly a Byzantine ally (p. 31), its seizure would be an essential preliminary to any attack on the centre of Byzantine power in the west, Sicily. And such an attack is precisely what Theophanes says Charles had in mind until, in 802, he instead proposed marriage (of the paper variety, naturally) to Irene. Her approval of this scheme, which would have united east and west, perhaps contributed to her deposition, in favour of Nicephorus, in 802.

However all this may be, the view that Charles, on entering St Peter's on Christmas Day, was unaware that a ceremony to make him emperor awaited is assuredly untenable. To mention one further point alone: Charles was acclaimed as emperor, with a devised formula at that; the acclaimers must have been rehearsed and the Franks could not have remained ignorant of this. No source can be construed as even hinting that Charles was taken by surprise. Save, that is, Einhard, who writes: 'It was at this time that he accepted the name of emperor and Augustus. This was something to which he was at first so greatly averse that he affirmed that he would not have entered the church that day, even though it was a principal festival, had he known the pontiff's intention beforehand.'

How is this to be explained? One thesis postulates that it was the *manner* of acquiring the imperial name which he disliked. Constitutionally, it was acclamation that made an emperor; coronation regularly followed but was strictly unnecessary. Charles himself became emperor by acclamation; this is why it is wrong to say he was 'crowned emperor' and misleading, at least, to speak of his 'imperial coronation'. However, he was certainly crowned first, acclaimed second. Leo, it is argued, deliberately reversed the normal order to foster the idea (which very quickly did become accepted) that papal coronation created the emperor. Charles's anger at the papal action explains Einhard's report and is reflected in his failure ever to return to Rome and his personal coronation of Louis in 813 (p. 47). There is value in this thesis, especially as regards Leo's aims, but it is flawed, both in particulars – for example, Leo and Charles often collaborated after 800 – and essentially, in that it does not account for Einhard. It accepts that Charles expected to receive the imperial name; and it is precisely the name to which Einhard reports him averse. Other suggestions will not be discussed. For the likeliest explanation by far is that Einhard gives us mere literary-moral cliché. Medieval men saw humility as a prime virtue of the ruler at any level; those who held authority therefore customarily presented themselves, and were presented by their admirers, as shunning appointment to office. (A relic of this attitude survives in the show of unwillingness to accept his post expected from a newly elected Speaker of the House of Commons.) Einhard is simply inviting his reader to note his hero's becoming modesty.

It was as emperor, then, that Charles left Rome shortly after Easter 801, to issue at Reno, on 29 May, the earliest surviving diploma bearing the formal title henceforth customary: 'Charles, most serene Augustus, crowned by God, great, pacific emperor governing the Roman empire and by the mercy of God king of the Franks and the Lombards'. Kingship, expressed in terms of peoples, had not been extinguished then; but alongside it stood territorial emperorship. The title 'emperor of the Romans' would have been inappropriately restrictive, and offensive to the bulk of his subjects, since 'Romans' to a westerner meant primarily the inhabitants of the city; hence 'governing the Roman empire', a formula of genuine imperial pedigree. Like his seal (p. 39) and his imperial coinage – the first based certainly on a coin, the second probably on a medallion, of Constantine – his title is irreconcilable both with the notion of an unwilling emperor and with that of the indifferent one whom some historians have detected in the post-coronation years.

The imperial years

Emperorship brought little or no increase in Charles's material power. But that does not mean that it was an empty distinction to him, without practical consequence. It is not that it involved specific responsibilities distinct from those of kingship. There was no sea-change after 800. Rather, it inspired an accentuation and intensification of the reforming theme already evident in the pre-imperial years. The goals of reform had not altered: order, justice, piety, peace, concord, each conceived in Christian terms, each expressive of God's will. But they were sought the more determinedly for Charles's consciousness of his great predecessors, of the lofty principles traditionally embraced in the idea of empire and of the expectations of God, Who had granted him the supreme dignity, Charles did not doubt, with a view to the advance of His cause. The more urgently too, no doubt, for awareness of passing years. Charles was nearly sixty in 800; time in which to better the account he must render God was drawing short.

Such considerations explain the remarkable reform enterprise which Charles launched on his return from Rome. Already in November 801 he summoned a synod to Aachen to look into the behaviour of the clerics. But the real starting point was another Aachen assembly, held in March 802, following which pairs of *missi* were sent out throughout the entire realm to do justice in allotted areas. These were bishops, abbots, dukes and counts, for the emperor chose, in the interests of the poor, not to use lesser men, palace vassals, who were more open to bribery. With them they carried written memoranda of instructions, these being based upon a document which was, as it were, a manifesto of Charles's imperial government and has accordingly been dubbed by Ganshof the 'programmatic' capitulary. If the *General Admonition* is the most earnest of Charles's capitularies, the programmatic capitulary is the loftiest. Wide-ranging, it is yet markedly religious in its general character. Moral offences loom large, and a block of fifteen clauses are devoted to clerical matters, where the themes are hierarchy, order and discipline. Perhaps uniquely, it reveals signs of Charles's personal intervention, for example in vehement first-person denunciations of incest, sodomy and murder. Charles's terrible awareness that God's judgement upon him will be conditioned by the conduct of his subjects is reflected in these clauses and several times made directly evident.

Two particular features should be noted. First, the scope of fidelity is greatly extended. The *missi*, who are to exact a new oath of fidelity to Charles as emperor, must explain publicly that this means more than an obligation to refrain from, and to disclose another's, active enmity towards him; it involves a duty not to harm churches, widows, orphans or strangers, not to pervert the course of justice, not to oppose his will or impede its execution, and much more. To strive to remain true to God is itself an obligation of fidelity, for Charles is responsible for his subjects' spiritual welfare yet 'cannot himself provide the necessary care and discipline for each man individually', as the capitulary almost plaintively puts it. This broadening of the notion of fidelity to embrace religious obligations and public duties is of considerable importance in the history of political thought.

Second, there is a pervasive concern to ensure that justice be done equitably and consistently. Men have the right to live under their 'national' laws but the *missi* must report unjust provisions for Charles's rectification. Injustices which they cannot correct must also be referred to him, in writing. There must be no subversion of the law; counts and other officers must have as assistants faithful servants of justice; perjury, 'the worst of crimes', is harshly treated. The judgement of numerous offences is reserved to Charles's own court. Most important, judges must judge in accordance with the written law, not at discretion. Nothing better illustrates Charles's aversion to the arbitrary.

Order was also the theme at a further Aachen assembly in October, where secular clergy, monks and laymen met separately. To the first was read and expounded the *Dionysio-Hadriana* (p. 22), to the second the Rule of St Benedict; the emperor then commanded that the members of each group must obey the appropriate body of norms, while all must follow the fathers. The business of the lay gathering, in which legal experts participated, was with the laws. One of the tasks of the *missi* of 802 had been to require every freeman to swear to the 'national' law by which he was ruled. At the October assembly these 'national' laws were read out and expounded; written emendations were made as necessary; and the emperor again declared that judges must follow the written law. It is in keeping with the concerns revealed here that Charles had certain previously unwritten 'national' laws recorded. The imperial tradition probably inspired this legislative emphasis, for it was emperors who stood as the supreme models of legislators.

It is impossible here to present even a summary account of the numerous further provisions of the imperial years, including the last great reform capitulary, that of Thionville in early 806. What must be said is that the themes already identified persist, that Charles's vision of a just and ordered Christian society beckoned him to the end. Its nobility is not lessened by the inevitability of its failure to materialize.

How, then, is Charles's decision in 806 – the very year a new, imperial, coinage was introduced – to provide for the posthumous partition of his territories among his three sons to be explained? Those historians who have seen in this decision proof of his hostility, indiference or disillusionment as regards the imperial title may seem to have a point. The relevant document, the *Division*, establishes the boundaries of three separate kingdoms and remains silent about the imperial title; the conclusion that it reflects the victory of traditional Frankish 'partition' thinking over the unitary concept of empire springs easily to mind. The truth is more subtle. As among the Romans, so among the earlier Franks, division implied no rejection of an overarching, single, political entity. Though two or more emperors or kings ruled independently, each with his own empire or kingdom, *the* empire, *the* kingdom of the Franks, survived notwithstanding. This was not just constitutional fiction. Analysis of the *Division* shows just what the Roman-imperial and Frankish precedents might lead us to expect: 'a scholarly dialectic between the ideas of partition and unity' (Folz). The infrequency of the word *imperium*, 'empire', as compared with *regnum*, normally rendered as 'kingdom', is not significant since *regnum* actually means 'an area ruled' and thus embraces *imperium*. The purpose of the *Division* was to avoid future, and probably current, hostility between Charles's sons by dividing 'the whole body of the *regnum*' between them; but 'the whole body' would not thereby cease to be. 'The kingdom . . . was to be a single whole, yet there were three kingdoms within it: our contemporary political vocabulary simply does not possess any term that would adequately describe this structure' (Folz). What Charles anticipated as regards the imperial title is a matter for speculation. But he considered that Leo should ratify the arrangements, as he duly did. Papal involvement does not support the view that these amounted to a rejection of the imperial concept.

Some historians have seen evidence of the importance to Charles of his imperial status in the outbreak of fighting with Constantinople, taking this as caused by his determination to force eastern recognition of his emperorship. Nothing suggests that he felt his title deficient without this or fought to secure it, though his status was naturally an issue in the peace negotiations. Only in 806 did the long-standing formal hostilities (p. 31) erupt into 'hot' war, and the cause was Charles's assumption of authority over Venetia and Dalmatia in response to overtures from the leaders of these nominally Byzantine territories. Nicephorus sent a fleet which recaptured both regions in 806–7, and another in late 808, following the expiry of a truce. But he was already seeking peace, and although the Venetian dukes – who had everything to lose, having betrayed both emperors – temporarily thwarted negotiations, in 810 an embassy arrived at Aachen. By then Venetia was again Frankish, but Charles returned it to Nicephorus, also handing over one of the treacherous dukes. Ratification of the peace was delayed until 815 for one reason and another. But in 812 the envoys of Michael I (811–13), on receiving the text of the treaty at Aachen, acclaimed Charles as emperor. It was the fifth century when Contantinople had last recognized another emperor. One's impression is that Charles was inveigled into this conflict and happy to extricate himself with diplomatic profit. Tactfully, he now omitted his formal title in writing to Michael, whom he called, as he called himself, 'emperor and Augustus'.

DECOMPOSITION?

Notwithstanding the above, Ganshof characterized the imperial years as a period of 'decomposition'. His judgement seems mistaken. Militarily, there was no noticeable decline. True, the days of outstanding offensive successes were past. But 'decomposition' is hardly the corollary of lack of expansion. In any case, there was territorial gain in Spain, where continuing interest after the 778 disaster is revealed by Gerona's acceptance of Frankish authority in 785 and a successful expedition down the Catalonian coast in *c.* 790. A Saracen raid of 793, undertaken in the belief that Charles was tied down by tough Avar resistance and resulting in the sack of the suburbs of Narbonne and a heavy defeat for the local forces, was a spur to fiercer endeavours. The facts are very difficult to establish. But by 814 the Franks seemingly had a firm grasp on the region down to Barcelona, itself taken in 801, held some areas to the west, including Pamplona, which had given allegiance in 806, and exercised a loose authority farther south. Although there had been failures, this was no mean achievement.

Nor was the warfare waged in the Mediterranean against raiders from Spain – and sometimes Africa – unsuccessful. A Moorish attack on the Balearics in 798 brought their voluntary submission to Charles, whose forces won a significant victory when the Moors returned in 799.

Further attacks, particularly on Corsica and Sardinia, punctuated the years up to 813, when the Moors also ravaged Civitavecchia, in Tuscany, and Nice. The nature of the hostilities did not permit a decisive defensive victory, and other Mediterranean commitments sometimes caused problems. Nevertheless, the reports suggest that Charles's men more than held their own. Naval power played an important role in this conflict, as it did in other campaigns. Charles was well aware of the value of fleets and the need for protection against those of others, as the capitularies, among other sources, indicate. Although the subject has not received the detailed examination it deserves, it is clear that 'the common picture of Frankish neglect of shipping and coastal defence is not borne out by the evidence of Charles's later years' (Bullough).

Naval power was a factor in the confrontation with Godofrid, king of the Danes, which began with the final settlement of the Saxon problem, itself belonging to the imperial years (p. 25). In view of Charles's record against pagans, and Danish succour to Saxon fugitives, past and current, one can understand the alarm of Godofrid, who in 804 assembled his forces on the Saxon border and was too fearful to attend a planned conference with Charles. Perhaps establishing the Abodrites north of the Elbe was intended to reassure him. In fact, it was not until 808 that Godofrid resorted to arms by attacking the Abodrites, who also faced their traditional enemies, the Wilzites. Though successful, he suffered heavily. But so did the Franks in an offensive against his Slav allies across the Elbe; Charles responded by building two fortresses on the river. Godofrid's awareness of the seriousness of his action is shown by his construction of a defensive barrier right across the neck of the Jutland peninsula, the Danewerk. The failure of a peace conference in 809 heralded escalation. Thrasco, the Abodrites' leader, aided by the Saxons, attacked the Wilzites and other allies of the Danes, only to meet assassination, while the Franks moved north of the Elbe with the construction of a stronghold on the Stör. In turn, Godofrid in 810 launched a great fleet at Frisia, where it enjoyed marked success, and threatened invasion of Saxony. Charles was now nearly seventy; nevertheless, he personally led a huge army into Saxony and, with naval support, awaited the promised onslaught. It never came; Thrasco's fate had befallen Godofrid also. The new king made immediate peace and on his death shortly afterwards the Danish kingdom fell victim to civil war, still unresolved when Charles died. 'Decomposition' is scarcely evidenced in this northern arena.

Other campaigns reveal similar vigour and no lack of success. Particularly noteworthy are the massive attacks on the Bohemian Slavs in 805 and 806, probably connected with an Avar prince's complaint of Slav harassment and request for resettlement – which was granted – early in 805. Avar–Slav disputes took one army to Pannonia in 811, while another engaged Slavs across the Elbe, and a third taught rebellious Bretons a lesson. All achieved their objectives. Next year the Wiltzites were forced to submission and the duke of Benevento to pay heavy tribute. At the end of his reign Charles's authority extended from the Atlantic to Hungary, from the North Sea to south of Rome, from beyond the Elbe to near the Ebro. Certainly his successor inherited external problems; how could it be otherwise, given such vast dominions? But the emperor had coped perfectly satisfactorily in his last years.

The argument for 'decomposition' from internal evidence is less easily rebuttable but more quickly dealt with. Essentially, it depends on the frequency with which Charles returned to the attack against his subjects' failure to live up to his demands. Does not the very repetitiveness of the denunciations and injunctions in the capitularies, the very constancy with which *missi* were dispatched, prove deterioration? In a word, no. While such an interpretation may be correct, it makes better sense to see in the phenomenon evidence of Charles's determination and sense of urgency (p. 42). Certainly the fact that, for example, corruption by the counts is a recurrent target of the later capitularies tells us nothing about its earlier prevalence. Nor does the appearance of shortcomings previously unmentioned prove the rise of new problems; indeed, one might argue that it rather shows the thoroughness and vigour of Charles's endeavours to seek out and eradicate all that was offensive in society.

In sum, Ganshof appears to have been uncharacteristically injudicious in championing the thesis of 'decomposition' in Charles's later years.

THE END

Charles's second son, Pippin, died in 810, the eldest, his namesake, in 811. He had relied increasingly upon them, and both had responded loyally. (Charles's excellent relations with his children should not be underrated as a factor in his success.) Louis alone was left, and in September 813, at Aachen, Charles crowned him before the magnates as his co-emperor, just as the Byzantine emperors sometimes crowned their intended successors. He had already made his will and devoted the time following, according to Thegan, to prayer, alms-giving and the correction of the gospels and other writings, according to Einhard, to hunting. Either activity would have been wholly in character. Early in the new year Charles contracted a fever. Dieting failed to help; pleurisy set in; and on 28 January the 'great and orthodox emperor, who nobly increased the kingdom of the Franks and reigned prosperously for forty-seven years', as his epitaph fittingly put it, died in his beloved Aachen.

No summary can begin to do justice to the vast scope of Charlemagne's activity, let alone to the immensity of his achievements and historical impact. From his time dates the transfer of the centre of European gravity from the Mediterranean, where it had always previously lain, to the north, where it has lain ever since. The vast dominion which he created – largely coincident with, and shaping the notion of, what we understand by 'Latin Christendom' – did not long survive as a political entity, it is true. But its very existence served to ensure that future Europeans could look back on a time when most of them had known unity; and the memory of this past association, coupled with certain common traditions which were in part its bequest and the high reputation which Charlemagne enjoyed, has contributed powerfully to the abiding strength of the unitary ideal among westerners. There is distant Carolingian blood in the EEC's vapid veins. No one with a smattering of knowledge of medieval or even of early modern times can fail to recognize the seminal importance of Charlemagne's re-establishment of a distinct western emperorship. The frequent involvement, for better or worse, of the emperors of the centuries ahead, overwhelmingly Germans, in Italian and papal affairs is ultimately a consequence of Charlemagne's seizure of the Lombard kingdom in 774 and assumption of the imperial title in 800. Germany itself could not have materialized as a political entity had not Charlemagne conquered and converted Saxony and absorbed Bavaria. The beginnings of the *Drang nach Osten*, the 'drive to the east', can reasonably be seen in his Avar and Slav wars; it was above all the Saxons, taking the Frankish mantle upon themselves and forcing the Slavs to Christianity as they themselves had been forced to it by him, who pursued this pressure in the tenth century. Further west, Charlemagne so effectively consolidated his father's achievement in Aquitaine that while the region was to retain its separate identity for centuries to come, it never rejected formal subjection to the kings of France. South of the Pyrenees the march centred on Barcelona survived, to give the region later known as Catalonia its permanent distinctiveness and to play an important role in the Christian reconquest of Spain, while Charlemagne's conflict with the Muslims came to be regarded and appealed to in future centuries as a prototype crusade.

Charlemagne was much more than a great warrior and conqueror, however. His educational endeavours and his fostering of intellectual life, touched on above, were manifestations of his driving passion: to create a truly Christian society. Harmony, order and justice, the constant themes of his capitularies, were pursued with such zeal because in Charlemagne's conviction they were what God, by entrusting him with government, had charged him to attain. Though the reign did see some important developments in the institutional field – the introduction of permanent judgement-finders in the courts, for example, and the much more extensive and regular use of *missi*, as direct representatives of the central government, to supervise the performance of its local officers – it witnessed no dramatic reforms in the administrative and governmental machinery. Charlemagne has been criticized for this, but it is not easy to discern quite what he might have been expected to do, given the prevailing state of communications and education and a land- rather than money-based economy. In any event, it was not through specific reforms but through the ethos he imparted to his reign and the reputation he left as a great Christian educator and patron of learning, law-giver and champion of justice, that Charlemagne made his impact upon the ages to come, for though the ideals he stood for and the notion of the ruler as responsible for all aspects of his people's welfare, spiritual and material, were not in themselves new, his renown ensured that they were endowed with a new strength, to live powerfully on in the mainstream tradition of western political thought. No less than his territorial achievement, his conceptual legacy moulded the shape of the European future.

Suggested reading

The best way to approach Charlemagne's reign is directly, through the sources. Both the original and the revised versions of the *AKF* are translated in my *Charlemagne: Translated Sources* (self-published, 1986: £6.75), which also contains numerous papal letters, capitularies and extracts from other annals, the relevant sections of the papal biographies and the Astronomer, and further material. While Alcuin is represented there, a very much fuller selection of his letters is given by Stephen Allott, *Alcuin of York* (York, 1974). Einhard's life is to be found translated by Lewis Thorpe in *Two Lives of Charlemagne* (Harmondsworth, 1969), where the other biographer is Notker the Stammerer. Potential readers should be warned against Thorpe's introduction, however, which is not only inadequately informed but often plain wrong.

The best general account of the reign is that by Donald Bullough, *The Age of Charlemagne* (2nd edn, London, 1973), though Robert Folz, *The Coronation of Charlemagne* (London, 1974), translated from the 1964 French text, ranges wider than the title suggests and is excellent. Heinrich Fichtenau, *The Carolingian Empire* (Oxford), 1968, reprint of 1957 edn), has worn well. The most recent English-language work dealing substantially with Charlemagne, Rosamond McKitterick, *The Frankish Kingdoms under the Carolingians* (Harlow, 1983) is sometimes helpful.

For the coronation see in addition to Folz (above), Richard E. Sullivan, *The Coronation of Charlemagne* (Boston, 1959), who provides an assortment of extracts representing different interpretations. Invigorating is Walter Ullmann, *The Carolingian Renaissance and the Idea of Kingship* (London, 1969). The last word is properly reserved for François Louis Ganshof, the most eminent of all scholars of Charlemagne's reign. His *Frankish Institutions under Charlemagne* (Providence, Rhode Island, 1968; also New York, 1970) and, especially, *The Carolingians and the Frankish Monarchy* (Harlow, 1971) – a collection of articles – are essential reading for anyone wishing to study Charlemagne's reign at all seriously.